KNOWING YOURSELF

KNOWING YOURSELF means being able to separate the true from the false in yourself — love from emotion, joy from sentiment, will from desire.

Does your life seem mechanical somehow? Do you look for something greater, in spite of yourself? Is what you've accepted as true, really the truth?

This book is like a window. First you catch sight of yourself in the false reflection of the glass. Then you look squarely at it. Finally you see through to the immaculate reality beyond.

BARRY LONG was born in Australia in 1926. For him the process of 'knowing yourself' began at the age of 31 and continued for several years. In 1965 he experienced a 'mystic death' and three years later came the transcendental realisation that marks the complete surrender of the false.

This book is a collection of the observations he made immediately following those critical phases of self-realisation. This is the seminal work of a man now regarded as a spiritual master and one of the most significant contemporary spiritual teachers to have emerged in the western world.

Knowing
YOURSELF

The true in the false

by

Barry Long

BARRY LONG BOOKS

This new, revised and extended edition first published 1996
by Barry Long Books
BCM Box 876, London WC1N 3XX, England.

Text first published 1969 in a private limited edition.
First published under the present title 1983.
Reprinted 1984, 1986, 1987, 1988, 1989.

Cataloguing-in-Publication Data:
A catalogue record for this book is available from The British Library.
Library of Congress Catalog Card Number: 96-090240.

ISBN 1 899324 03 8

Printed in England on acid-free paper by Redwood Books.
Cover design: Rene Graphics, Brisbane.
Cover photo: courtesy of Gem Studies Laboratory, Sydney.
Photo of Barry Long: Ambyr Johnston, 1996.

BARRY LONG BOOKS are published by The Barry Long Foundation
an educational charity registered in the United Kingdom.
Distributed in the United States by
ATRIUM PUBLISHERS GROUP
3356 Coffey Lane, Santa Rosa, California 95403.

CONTENTS

preface

THIS BOOK IS about you and it is all true. It contains no theories and no arguments. But you must not believe me for I might be a liar or a fool.

No man can teach another self-knowledge. He can only lead him or her up to self-discovery — the source of truth. You must not believe anyone in the search for truth; you have to find out for yourself. But although you are on your own, help will come when it is really needed.

You are either ready to discover yourself or you are not. Ready means you have been knowingly or unknowingly practising self-observation.

The book is an experience in energy. It is not a book about knowing yourself: to read it is knowing yourself. If you are ready it is going to disturb you. You are going to feel elevated, excited, confused, uncertain, irritated, resentful, hostile or even physically agitated. All these are normal reactions in different personalities to the energy which is released during the process of knowing yourself.

If when you finish reading the book you feel left up in the air, wondering what it was all about or what you should do next to know yourself better, then read it again, and again; and gradually, or in a flash, you'll find the solution.

You don't gather knowledge when you are getting to know yourself; you lose it. Many of your firmest ideas go out the window. You may feel naked, vulnerable, threatened, argumentative, angry. But if you are really looking for the truth and not for some personal vindication you will start to discover you have access to the same source of truth as the wisest teachers who ever lived.

Truth is of the moment, never of the man. And 'man' as I use the word includes all of us, men, women and children.

It is a little known fact that truth cannot be memorised. Truth has to be discovered now, from moment to moment. It is always fresh, always new, always there for the still, innocent mind that has experienced life without needing to hold on to what has gone before.

This Edition

Earlier editions included only the material in the first seventeen chapters. They were written in 1965 following my first significant spiritual realisation. Three years later came a second stage and around the same time I wrote another manuscript. The present edition is based on both original manuscripts, revised and rearranged.

There are now five 'steps' in the book. Each step contains six short chapters. With each chapter you approach yourself from a different angle.

Absorb what is said as you read but endeavour not to hold on to it or think about it. Read in the moment and each step will take you closer to complete self-knowledge.

ONE

TO KNOW YOURSELF COMPLETELY IS TO HAVE experienced being God and to have access at any moment to the truth this tremendous experience reveals.

The experience gives the continuous certainty of being responsible for every moment of your life: that whatever happens, the good, the bad and the indifferent, is your own will.

Within this all-sustaining knowledge is the unquestionable certainty of immortality; but at the same time it is also possible to experience responsibility for the immediate environment and finally for the entire universe including the earth's apparent discord of war and suffering.

What I have just described is not intellectual possibility but living experience — more intense in its reality and perception than the experience of being alive.

But you must not believe me. You must realise it in yourself, know it, for it is beyond words and thinking. And it has to be experienced without recourse to drugs or insanity.

Then you must live your knowledge; be your knowledge. For truth is for all men and women, not just for yourself.

the robot mind

THE FIRST BARRIER to self-knowledge is that man thinks like a machine: we are for or against, or switched off, not interested. No one wants to listen; everyone wants to talk.

We are a world of robot thinkers programmed by robot parents, robot teachers and a robot society. We know little outside what someone else has taught us or said. The little else we think we know we churn out with a monotony that sends us rushing to television, pop music or alcohol to drown our own screeching mediocrity.

Every generation of youth seems to sense it and tries to rebel. But to change the robot world we must first change the robot patterns of our own inherited thinking. Revolution without this fundamental change is the substitution of one evil for another — precisely what man has been doing for thousands of years. The young rebels soon put out their wrists contritely to be chained to the rest of the shuffling, mechanical throng.

To be different permanently, and not be a misfit or an eccentric, you must first understand what has to be changed. This is what self-knowledge is all about.

The robot in us is clearly the enemy. It is the cause of most of the worry, suffering and unhappiness in everybody's life. It is the thing we have to understand by becoming conscious — by observing our own mind in action.

People are unconscious for most of their lives and they seldom see themselves as they are, except by accident. When they do they usually run from the fact in horror. They sleep from birth to death, enmeshed in the robot's thinking which they imagine is themselves.

You must not believe this. To believe what another says about you is unconscious, robot thinking. Nothing is true in self-discovery unless it is true in your own experience. This is the only protection against the robot levels of the mind.

Truth does not need argument, agreement, theories or beliefs. There is only one test for it and that is to ask yourself 'Is the statement true or false in my experience?'

The ability to distinguish between true and false depends on your understanding of yourself which in turn depends on how long and how often you are able to remain aware of yourself. Any source claiming to teach you truth or wisdom has to be tested in this way. Truth cannot be taught but it is quickly recognised by the person ready to discover it.

There are two kinds of knowledge. One is worldly knowledge, the knowledge of things outside yourself — what you learned at school, how to drive a car, your work, every activity that makes up the world's and your daily life. This practical side of living gives varying degrees of success, wealth and fame. It produces cleverness, business acumen, lots of words and good advice; but it cannot produce real wisdom.

The other knowledge is self-knowledge — the knowledge of relationships, of fear, desire and all the emotions that make up the self in us.

The robot mind manages to mix these two worlds into an amazingly convincing confusion that leads man nowhere.

Self-knowledge reveals rather startling facts. When these are faced you begin to discover what is true and what is false in the world.

If you think you know yourself you are wrong. If you think you know what is true and false in the world you are wrong. Neither do the other five thousand million know, or there would be no worry. Yet everybody worries — because everybody thinks the same.

If you look at your aims you will find they represent the desire for power, position, prestige, possessions (including people) and permanence (to hold what you have). The desire for success in any of these aspects is really the desire for power.

Everyone pursues them in one form or another in the belief that their fulfilment will result in happiness or contentment. They won't of course, and our terrible inner contradiction is that we secretly realise it.

We know we are only happy for a while no matter what we attain. We are happy with a promotion which offers the prospect of more success in the future, more money now, and immediate prestige. But if we fail to be promoted next time, or have to wait too long, we will be unhappy.

Real happiness and contentment must be a constant, unchanging state that does not depend on the swinging pendulum of success or failure. But everyone keeps chasing the same things because the robot mind cannot pause long enough to look for a source of happiness beyond acquisition.

Am I telling you to give up your ambitions, to give up the desire for success, fame and fortune? No. Get out there and acquire the whole world if that is what you want. Out there in the thick of it is the easiest place to discover yourself. No aim, no ambition is too high if you have it. Do not let others infect you with their deadening fear and curb your desire for glory and attainment. Get out there if you can and be one of the few in every generation who clamber above the heads of the masses and wave their hands with a laugh shouting 'Look at me, World. I made it!'

But on the way up see that you stay conscious, aware of what you are doing. It is the conscious man or woman who finds the secret of happiness and contentment; and that, surely, is the ultimate success.

To listen, to learn, your mind has to be still.

Have you ever observed that you can have only one thought in your mind at a time? If you are sitting down planning what clothes to take on holiday your mind is on selecting them. If someone asks where you are going that afternoon the holiday planning has to go out of your mind so it can be directed onto the afternoon programme. While you are thinking you cannot listen or absorb anything because your only avenue of awareness is occupied.

Can you listen when you judge? Can you learn anything? Or do you only receive your own worn-out opinions, the product of a tiny bit of life you happen to have experienced or read about?

If you are told that most of the time you are unconscious it is the habit of the mind to immediately judge and declare, 'That's silly. I am conscious. I know I am conscious. If I were unconscious I would not be able to do these things.' But if your response is 'That may be so', you are in a state of receptivity and ready to receive what is new.

The still, receptive mind begins with the state of 'I do not

know so I will listen.' The busy, rigid mind begins with 'I
believe' or 'I do not believe' — with judgment and opinions.

The movement each day is for your opinions to grow stronger
and more numerous. This is especially true of youth as the robot
thinkers gradually sew them up in a cocoon of imagined rights
and wrongs and good and bad which all proclaim yet ignore
when it suits them — and are insulted if told so.

To break through you have to be in a constant state of
listening, for truth is discovered at the most unusual and
unexpected times. You have to resist the terrible, crushing, at
times almost unbearable pressure of the robot world about you
that will do anything — expose you to hate, vilification, tears,
ridicule, taunts of insanity, even psychological crucifixion — to
make you conform to its way of thinking, get back into line and
join the dead who bury the dead.

The pursuit of self-knowledge takes increasing courage. Not
the kind of courage that impresses with its daring, but an inner
courage that if you have it will eventually give you willpower.

While the mind sees things through opinion and judgments (and
it will as long as they are there) you can never see what is true.
For example, the belief that God does or does not exist has to
be discarded. You don't know. That is the fact. But you can find
out through self-knowledge.

The robot minds will try to convince you God does or does
not exist, that you should believe even though it is self-evident
that you cannot believe anything by an act of will. You have to
know to believe; and then you do not have to believe — you
know.

Half the world says God exists, the other half disagrees. One
of them is wrong. You might believe the wrong one. To believe

either is robot thinking because neither knows.

When self-knowledge reveals the answer it will be a living fact in your own experience. At any time you wish to experience the answer it will be there, just as you can say 'It is night' or 'It is day'. You will know, while the rest of the world is arguing and speculating.

From this point on you have to discard your opinions of whether another person's behaviour is good or bad. You can judge no one because you will always perceive them through the slightest distortion of your judgment. Where strong emotion is involved it is not unusual for you to see only your own judgment and not the person at all. And there is always the terrible possibility you might be wrong.

The point of this is that while you are concerned with an opinion about a person you cannot listen and might miss the truth. If someone offends you, then you can avoid him as much as possible (which you already do anyway) but without thinking about it. Judging someone to another person is this kind of thinking in words. It is the heartbeat of the robot mind.

Man will give an opinion on almost anything. He does not stop to observe that most of the time he is repeating what someone else has said or written and what he has chosen to believe. He takes other people's ideas as his own or rejects them outright according to his conditioning.

The first conditioning we are exposed to, irrespective of community or race, is that we are the body. Then, that we are individuals. Neither can be proved. But we are not going to draw any conclusions, for he who looks and looks long enough must find the truth.

What are you? Every answer to this question comes from the robot mind which lies like a great brick wall between us and the truth. Every answer it gives us about ourselves is but another question, a reaction bouncing back off the same superficial knowledge, an amalgam of what we already know. So we get all the answers but no solutions.

The only way we can ever get through to the truth is by finding out what we are not. We do that by looking, by observation. It is by observing we are not the objects around us that we get our sense of duality, our self-consciousness. So by observing the robot mind in action we gradually disidentify from it and finally realise we are something else. That something — consciousness without the self — is beyond the reactions of the robot and it is there we find the truth.

The robot in us is memory. Worry, fear, every thinking reaction comes out of memory. This must be understood first. You can demonstrate this to yourself now by asking yourself a question, any question, and following what happens.

You must forget any theories you have read or heard. We are not concerned with intellectual thinking or arguments here. You do not need to know psychological terms, what Freud said and the rest of it.

This process of self-discovery is scientific and the invariable rule of science has to be applied — experiment and observe. The experiment is to ask the question; the observation is to look at yourself and see what happens. Being a science the laws cannot vary. Any apparent variation is in you: you will have stepped off the way of facts into conclusions. The sun is either shining or it is not. You do not have to conclude; you just look.

When a research scientist enters his laboratory to try to

discover something new he leaves outside all his opinions, likes and dislikes. He sets up his experiment, begins the action and observes the results. You have to be a scientist, observing the challenge that life throws up. The beauty of it is that the experiment is always working. You do not have to set aside time or interfere with any of your activities. The hardest part is to make sure the scientist, the observer of yourself, is there.

Sometimes as you peer into the magnificent unexplored depths of yourself, your very being will sing at the beauty of a truth discovered and you will exclaim with all the triumph and certainty of a scientist, 'That is right.' But do not imagine you can share your jubilation with everyone. Unless they are explorers of themselves they will not understand. They may say they do but they cannot, and you will know they do not. The rewards in this process go only to those who make the effort; that is the superb justice of it.

Memory is the product of experience and it contains the facts you use to cope with the practical side of life. But it must also contain something else, otherwise we would all agree on the facts and there would be no dispute. You cannot sensibly argue about how many legs a cow has, yet our lives are spent in almost continual dispute and disagreement.

People have wagered their lives on something as precarious as their memory of a date. We do it in a smaller way every time we have an argument. People declare with massive all-excluding conviction that such-and-such a thing is true. 'I know it is,' they cry. Who knows it is? On what immovable ground do these great declarations of truth rest? On impressions.

The greatest part of memory consists of impressions. These are the results of conditioning — the religion we were brought up in, our political, family and social environment. It is the most subtle, cloying form of all experience. Impressions are the source of all our opinions and arguments.

When you say God does or does not exist, or that someone is good or bad, you are drawing on impression-memory. When you say you 'feel' or 'just know' something, you are using impressions. It is unscientific to say you 'feel' something. It really means you have not made the effort to find out the fact.

When you next reply 'I don't know' to a question, observe the state of no-thought, the absence of busy reference to memory, to conditioning and impressions. You are like a photographic plate exposed in a darkroom, absolutely still yet perfectly poised to receive the light, the new.

the fact

YOU STOPPED BELIEVING in fairy stories when you found out that magic wands were not a fact of life in your experience. But in the days when you listened to them you were not so sure. As a child you did not have sufficient life experience to prove them false.

Children do not listen to fairy tales for entertainment or escape. They live them, and believe them as though they were life itself. The developing mind is so devised that before reading and writing occurred, even before the advent of language, it apprehended all experience in living. With language occurred the first corruption, the first lies and the first fairy tales. So children continue to believe such things are true until life itself proves them to be false.

You can make children believe anything, even that you are magical and wise, but your pose is doomed because life will instruct them by experience that you have deceived them and are not wise; and eventually they will not listen to you or consult you. Later, having failed as grown-ups to find wisdom in them-selves, they will pretend to their own children that they are wise, with the same tragic results.

Self-knowledge is the process of becoming de-hypnotised. When you are hypnotised you see things as they really are not, mistaking the false for the true. A self-deluding process is required — a robot imagination.

Without imagination man would not be man, yet it is the main obstacle to self-knowledge. The trouble begins when we allow imagination to use us, and this occurs whenever it draws images from the impressions in the memory. Then we suffer. And if we use our misery to observe ourselves we discover that this type of imagination is the curse of man, the thing that separates us from God, if there is a God.

Impressions in the memory are the cause of most of the pain and misery in your life and everyone else's. But the memory also contains facts. With impression-memory man argues. With factual memory he gets things done.

The world progresses materially through the use of facts. From medicine to spaceships, every new device and practical service to mankind has its origin as a progressive development of factual memory. Man always uses it in his work or when there is something important to do. But as soon as he finishes work he switches over to impression-memory. This emotional memory is where he keeps his imaginings of the significance of experience, of what he is and what others are. Here he is no longer concerned with facts. He enters the world of imagination and opinions — the world of the false. And yet when he has an important job to do, when he cannot afford to fail, he deals only in facts.

Countless men and women have contributed in their own way to progress but have contributed not one fact to answer the question 'Where am I going? What's it all about?' Are the ones who came before you your hypnotists? Are you in turn the hypnotist of your children? There is only one way to find out. You have to see yourself exactly as you are — not as you imagine you are.

When you observe yourself you must not condemn or approve what you see. If you tell a lie there is no need to judge yourself. The judge cannot be the judged, and even to accept is to judge. The fact is that you lied. There is no need to tell anyone else, just face the truth alone.

As you continue watching yourself you will observe that you are an habitual liar. Even recounting a simple happening you will observe yourself lie or exaggerate for no reason. If you try to find a reason you are judging again, trying to justify.

You will be amazed at what you see. The scientist when he is observing the results of an experiment is often amazed at what he sees; and he can laugh at it too, without changing the results.

If you try to change what you see you have failed again. To succeed in any endeavour you have to keep coming back to your object. Your object is to see yourself exactly as you are. You are not just a liar; you are many other disagreeable things. If you try to change them all you will not have time to know yourself or change yourself; and then you will be back with all the others before you who tried to change themselves but never succeeded. If we could easily change things by opposing them what a mess we would be in. What is good to some is bad to others. Some would change the good; others would change the bad.

There is no escape from the old in the old, or we would all be free. Self-knowledge is the discovery of the new: it looks beyond the world that has all the answers and no solutions.

You buy a diamond ring. It costs a lot of money and for years you wear it with the satisfaction that goes with owning something beautiful or valuable. One day an expert proves that it's a worthless imitation. Do you continue to wear it with the same pleasure? No. You discard it. You leave it in the drawer or let your children play with it.

The truth is that once you discover something is false you lose interest in it. Man no longer treasures what he thought was genuine once he discovers it is false. In this way truth is its own solution.

Self-knowledge is the discovery of the false. You do not have to find what is true: when the false is discarded truth is there. It always was.

Just keep observing the fact and the change will come automatically and will be lasting. When you discover you are a liar and face the fact without excuses you will begin to stop lying. Lying will drop away like a dead leaf that is no longer part of the tree.

You are also a hypocrite. You are cruel, selfish, greedy and envious. You do not live up to the standards of behaviour and thought you profess and expect of others. You allow yourself the indulgence of anger but condemn it in others. You will cheat in a business deal and excuse it as business. You will defame another man or woman to amuse yourself in conversation and then go home and say you love. If that is love there is no hope. Love, if it exists, must be constant and not the plaything of inconstancy.

When the link between one fact and another is not apparent, remember that life is always moving and do not separate the part from the whole.

Life is a stream sweeping you along and the facts are like immovable rocks in the middle of the stream. Face each fact as it presents itself and rest. The stream will carry you around and beyond. Struggle away from the fact by not facing it and you fight against the stream of life and suffer. It is the law. There is no other way.

To face a fact is to look at it full on, no matter how ugly or painful it is. Then it dissolves and like the smashed atom releases a tremendous energy which we apprehend as the moment of decision or the moment of truth.

A man wants to find out what is in the valley over the hill. He climbs to the top of the ridge and looks. At first he sees only what is, as it is — the valley and all that is in it. He does not say the river at the north end should be at the south. He does not say what should be and what should not be. He looks. Then he has the desire to live there. But the desire is not the fact; it is only the path leading up to the fact.

When he actually goes to live in the valley the things he can change about it can be changed. But it is the fact that they are capable of being changed that changes them; the man is merely the instrument. If the water can be diverted he will face the fact and do it. He does not have to judge anything as long as he keeps facing the facts.

If the river is too far away to irrigate his fields, and it cannot be diverted, the man will have to face the fact, perhaps even weep with frustrated desire and go elsewhere. If he does not face the fact, and moves into the valley on the strength of his desire and its blind optimism, he will be living in imagination, dreamland with reality's agony; and life will become a lingering misery.

The fact comes first. It is always that way, but this truth cannot be seen unless the mind is very still. In the beginning you may only glimpse it.

Why is it that most magazines devote the front page to a picture of a pretty girl, although she may not be connected with the contents? And why is she always smiling, looking happy or sexy?

The answer may seem obvious to the robot mind but that does not mean it is really understood. The device would not work if everyone saw through it. The fact is that the manufacturers and advertising men who deal in these things aim to create a desire for their products by planting the alluring impression in your mind that they are bringing you happiness. This works because real happiness is not known. If it was, even to suggest that a magazine could cause it would be ridiculous. It might make you laugh to be tickled with a feather, but that doesn't mean the feather causes happiness. And laughter is not the indicator of happiness, as we all know.

People imagine happiness is associated with possessions, whether money, houses, cars, television sets, pretty girls or handsome men. They never cease imagining this even though in their own experience the happiness of possession inevitably wilts and droops. So the false is tolerated and believed because the fact is not faced and is therefore powerless to bring the new.

Our object here is to discover what is false. By observation we have discovered that imagination is false when it separates the part from the whole and builds on only one aspect of a fact — an impression. So if you separate yourself from this imagining you separate yourself from the false.

When you identify with imagining you identify with the false and you are unconscious robot thinking. When you are identified with a state you are that state. When your thinking is unreal, so are you. When you are angry, you are anger.

You can never stop anger by decision. Anger is the same monster every time. Its energy is emotion and emotion is the result of conflict. Conflict comes from robot imagining and that is the result of trying to change 'what is' without facing the fact.

Anger, like all the other corrupting identities in you, has to be observed and understood and then it disintegrates and never returns. You cannot be anger and the observer at the same time, but you can appear to be angry and still be the observer. It takes tremendous power to remain the observer under provocation. But anger, being false, cannot exist in the spotlight of intelligent observation.

the need of love

TO SEE WHAT is good for other people first requires a great amount of work on yourself. The truth, which is the real good, can be discovered only in relation to yourself. To do this the mind has to be very still.

Stored away in your impression-memory is what you imagine to be good for you and the various people in your life, for humanity, for the world and all things generally. But you do not even know the truth in relation to yourself yet. To see the truth in relation to someone else is absolutely beyond your capability.

Our attempts to live together are a constant collision of everyone's imaginings of what everyone's needs are. You do not know the fact about yourself or them; and they do not know the fact about themselves or you. What a circus.

'Why can't I find happiness? Why are there quarrels, greed, murder, suicides, wars? Why can't people live together in harmony? Why am I never really content, no matter what I acquire, whether it be man or woman, gold or power?'

It is quite simple. You do not know your need, and you will never know it unless you know yourself. You see all needs through the eyes of the ephemeral robot, not understanding that the purpose of need is the need of life to experience itself as a totality beyond the apparent individual needs of men and things. So there is the mystery of death and destruction and birth and life; a structural justice, an integrity of opposites, a being of all things called immortal life.

You still imagine another's need like a do-gooder (and that includes all of us at some time) or the professional reformers who will reform anything except themselves. Do-gooders and professional reformers never solve anything. They work on the outside — on what appears to be a need. They deal in appearances, not understanding that every appearance is an expression of a cause beyond itself. They relieve a pocket of poverty in the mighty garment of the world, but only for a moment in the majesty of its years. When they discover a more needy cause everything they touch falls back to what it was. They sometimes leave bitterness and misery behind, for those they fed will hunger again and those they saved will fall again. They have given of their time, perhaps of their possessions, but not of themselves.

You cannot give what you do not know, or you are not the giver. And what is it to give of your possessions? One day you may lose them and have nothing to give.

Love is beyond description; but not beyond demonstrating. For the moment you must forget anything you ever thought you knew about love. If you look through the screen of the old you cannot understand and you will not be listening.

You cannot love a person, a thing or an event. But you can be in the state of love in relation to it. Then you are the object's need or it is your need, and your love will continue; but only as long as the need lasts.

If the object does not or cannot know itself, it might not consciously recognise its love. An example of this is the air you breathe. It is in a state of love in relation to you. It is your need and without it you will die. You are not consciously in a state of love with it. But when you know yourself, you will be. For you to know your love (air) someone has to put a pillow over your head. When the pillow is removed you go back to sleep, which you call living, oblivious of the delight of knowing this love.

You are alive according to your knowledge of love.

Love is choiceless, just as the air has no choice but to support your life and you have no choice but to breathe it.

In the state of love you have to be creative: you have no choice and you want none.

A real reformer is a person in love. He has no choice: he acts because he cannot do otherwise.

Love is beyond the mind because it is always new.

The mind draws only on the past, on your experience and on the experience of others which is stored in memory, books or records of some kind. Any product of the mind is a reaction of the past, a synthesis of what is old. So the mind is a modifier, a reactor, a renovator, but it cannot create the new.

The composer of a new melody creates no new notes on the piano. The new combination of notes was already there in the potential of the keyboard. When the most gifted composers and writers, the leading architects and most original designers create, their minds are in a state of stillness or meditation on their love. And out of the silence, the beyond, into the silent waiting mind comes the fulfilment of the need, the fact, the refreshing new that sets the rest of the poor, mediocre, thinking world agog with its brilliance and genius.

The mind cannot know love. Where there is thought, love is not. When the robot mind is active it thinks all the time and is the master. When the robot mind is mastered, undisciplined thinking ceases and is replaced by awareness.

Awareness can know love. You can only experience the new when you are aware, when you are without thought. However we are seldom still enough to know what we love, especially in relation to the work we do. Even if we knew we would probably choose the career that seemed to promise success and money. Thus in our jobs we are mostly unhappy or only reasonably happy (which means dissatisfied) and we are mostly mediocre and uncreative in them.

Man's needs are ever being filled, therefore ever changing. When a need is filled there is no longer any need. That is why love as we know it never seems to last. But it is not the love that changes; it is the need.

It is the action of the mind to cling to what it has known even though the fact is that there is no need. The mind has read and heard that love is for ever; and imagines it is. It wants so much to be creative, but never can be.

Love is for ever, invariable and changeless, but not in relation to any object. For all things have a need and when that need is satisfied the love that provided it must change and appear as another need.

The final need is love itself. So if you loved something as your one remaining need you would have to die. Not 'die for', which is the robot mind's imagination of the ultimate in love, but 'die into'. Then you would be one — no lover, no beloved.

Love's movement is always towards union. It is the unifier of creation, the destroyer of division.

giving

IF YOU LOOK at life's totality you will notice that every living thing exists for something else. Each organism is like a tunnel. At one end it receives: at the other it gives. In between it converts what it has received into a form suitable for another organism to receive. This giving and receiving is not done by choice; it is choiceless. There has to be giving as there has to be receiving.

The failure to give and receive is followed first by unconsciousness and then death. If you would try to stop anything giving or receiving, by the same action you will summon to it unconsciousness or death. For unconsciousness is the next to last need of all things with a brain, and death is the final need of all unconscious life.

Why is it that so often when you give to another with a generous smile and gesture at the same time you feel the stab of selfishness and know you really do not want to give?

Why is it when someone gives to you that you often notice your torrent of thanks doesn't carry the sincerity you verbally express? That for a strange, almost frightening reason you are not moved at all; and could just as easily take and walk away?

Under the unbreakable law of the universe you have to receive what you need, and what you need is not what you imagine you need. Here is the tide that knows no individual. Your mind will always come up with a reason for giving or receiving. It will say you wanted to, or that you were a fool to give and won't do it again. But in the massive sweep of life the fact remains that you had no choice.

When your mind imagines what you need or imagines that you are giving out of choice, at that moment you can experience in yourself the lie of hypocrisy. For that moment, if you see it, you are conscious.

You go through the act of gratitude because your mind says 'Everyone would be grateful in the same position.' Gratitude is, but it is beyond the robot mind — although not beyond experiencing.

Gratitude is a state that can only exist when the giver gives because he would die if he did not; and the receiver receives because he would die if he did not. In the moment neither of them thinks or speaks, or feels he is the giver or the taker, and the experience is sacred because in the moment both receive love.

All life begins with the sun. The sun shines and gives of itself: it has no choice. Heat from the sun evaporates water, clouds build up and when they become too heavy it rains and they give of themselves. The air must give of itself to man's body as breath, and man in breathing converts the oxygen to carbon dioxide to give it to the trees so that they can breathe their need and in living convert it back to oxygen so that man's body may breathe again. The earth must give of itself to the trees and grass and they give of themselves to the animals and birds who give of themselves to man. And when all things die they must go back to feed the earth; and the earth receives and gives so that all things can receive and give — none has a choice.

Of all created things, man alone possesses the potential to give by choice the thing that all creation is waiting for, the thing that only man can give — the awakened state of consciousness.

To give consciousness is simply a matter of becoming conscious, of waking up. But man would separate mankind from the rest of creation and contribute nothing consciously except to himself. Although he has received from creation and is capable of giving it the most precious gift of consciousness, its final need, he chooses not to give it; and so, by contributing nothing through his life except to himself, he perpetuates self-ishness and ignorance on the planet.

Life's penalty for not giving or receiving consciously is unconsciousness. So man like all things is unconscious. As unconsciousness is the next to last need of all things with a brain, and death the final need of all unconscious life, so all unconscious life is mortal, including man the way he is.

When man rediscovers the truth of choicelessness he begins to know himself; he begins to wake up, become conscious. He begins to see life as it is and not as he dreams it to be in the unconscious condition of thinking and imagining. He begins to give, and the more man gives in the selfless endeavour to know himself, the more conscious he becomes.

Man conscious is man immortal. Man conscious gives to the creation as no other thing can give and is beyond death.

But it is no use my just saying this. You must discover it, realise it for yourself.

the mars element

ASTROLOGY IS STUDIED as a predictive science: it is believed that the nine planets which revolve with the earth around the sun govern the lives of everyone and that the future can be foretold from the positions they will occupy. Astrologers have made some amazingly accurate predictions and countless blunders.

According to astrology each planet possesses certain characteristics that cause specific events in people's lives. Round and round the planets go and because they are at a certain point in the sky in relation to their position when you were born, you hit your thumb with a hammer, get off on the wrong foot with your new boss, no longer make progress despite increased efforts, win a lottery or get a pay rise.

We are not concerned with astrology, but it contains principles we can use in the study of ourselves. What I am leading up to is a device to help you keep awake, conscious, while the robot minds around you snore on, imagining they know. But remember the mind will fight you all the way, with judgments and opinions about what is being said, and if you give in you will be unconscious again.

We will look at the principles of just three planets: Mars, Saturn and Jupiter. As you become more conscious you will be able to see the principles of these planets at work in your life.

The astrologers say Mars is a fiery energetic planet that causes accidents, violence, fire, blood, hate, war and anger. Mars is quick and hurts like a punch on the nose.

Saturn is a slow-moving planet that causes misery, sorrow, poverty, sullenness and delay.

Jupiter is the opposite to Mars and Saturn. It is the great giver of good. It is good luck, the fortunate occurrence, success, the unexpected win, the end of delay, the miraculous escape and so on. It is a Mars situation when a plate slips out of your hand, and a Jupiter one when you catch the plate an inch from the ground.

But strangely, good fortune is like an injection of morphine; it puts you into a deeper sleep. That is why a man once said it is easier for a camel to pass through the eye of a needle than for a rich man to enter the kingdom of heaven. A rich man has much to lose before he really suffers and turns inward.

Let us look at life in relation to the Mars and Saturn elements. Very few, if any, of the things we attempt go according to our expectations. Not only big things but everything. The things that go wrong are the Mars and Saturn elements in life. (I will refer to them from now on just as the Mars element.) The robot mind treats these things as separate from life, as unconnected happenings that interfere with or spoil the enjoyment of living. They are bad luck, bad news, a sad event, a cruel blow, a setback. They cause worry, tears, anger, rejection, fear, discontent — most of the feelings that are opposite to the feelings of happiness and contentment.

If the Mars element were absent you would merely desire something and it would be yours. There would be no interference, no competition, nothing to overcome, nothing to deflect you; no sorrow, no challenge, no disappointments, no accidents, no hospitals, no pain, no debt, no death.

Do you see the absurdity of this division? Follow its thinking through and you mentally destroy the fact of life and create what must be paradise. But life is the fact; or do you deny it?

Whenever the Mars element strikes, you are upset in varying degrees. Whenever it appears to be absent, you are happy or undisturbed. If the Mars element were absent forever, and everything were to go smoothly, you might imagine it would be the secret of happiness and contentment. That is obvious. But as we have seen, to experience that state would destroy living as the robot mind knows it. The only alternative is to accept everything that happens as a part of life and not react to it. That would be the practical secret of happiness and contentment.

The robot mind pursues everything it sets out to do with the attitude that there will be no interference from the Mars element; that life will actually suspend the essence which is its existence. You might say that people expect things to go wrong. That is saying it, not living it. If you have the mental attitude that acknowledges the ever-present possibility of the Mars element, you can never get angry or upset when it strikes.

You get in a friend's car and smash the wing as you drive up the street. Your reaction is a degree of worry, anguish or fear. You are shocked when Mars strikes, otherwise you would have no reaction.

Look at this closely; but do not look for contradictions. If you see the main fact, then the side-issues that your mind wants to raise will become clear. The mind is your greatest enemy. Its very function is to keep the truth hidden.

You smash the car and suffer worry. But if you were

conscious of the presence of the Mars element, you could not worry. To worry, or suffer mentally about the fact of life, is ridiculous. Why not worry about all the other people who smashed their cars today? — all those who will lose a limb, the children who will be crippled, the fifty thousand who will die of starvation. Why not worry about everything else in life that life itself will afflict today? You cannot worry about it all, can you? That's impossible.

Worry is a purely selfish expression. The fact is that to worry or suffer mentally you have to have an opinion. You have to say 'That is bad in relation to me.' The opinion will prevent you from seeing the truth.

When you smash the car the only fact in your experience is that the car is smashed. It is your judgment that it is 'bad'. You might say that most people, especially the owner, will agree with you that it is bad. But no; they will not. The smash will be good for the man who repairs the car and for those he employs: without car-smashes and breakdowns they would be out of work. It will be good for the company who makes the spare parts and if the car is a write-off it will be good for the car manufacturers and all the people who work for them. You may imagine it is bad for the insurance company; but it will be good for the bank which provides the insurance company's overdraft at a profit out of which it pays wages. It will be good for the Post Office and office workers because it will involve letters, documents, stamps, phone calls, and so on. In fact it appears to be bad only for the owner, the insurance company and you. But the insurance company exists because of the profits it makes on such risks, and if there were no accidents there would be no insurance companies. So it is not bad for the company.

For the owner, the smash is the Mars element, which is life, and he judges that life is bad because the smash is bad for him. For the Mars element to be eliminated from his life it must be eliminated from all lives and that would be the end of life.

Yet, like you and everyone else, he wants to eliminate the bad from his life.

Life is composed of the coming and going of money. What money is spent on does not matter. The bloodstream of your life is the coming and going of money. Some things, like smashes, do seem unnecessary, but this is because you live on the surface. Has anyone ever succeeded in avoiding such things?

The movement of money is a total act of life and not of the individual. It is like the tide; it sweeps out leaving behind numberless small puddles of various capacities which it will destroy or refill when it flows in again. All of life depends on this constant, regular movement, and the mass of little puddles which contain the full tide must give back continuously so that the puddles on the other side of life can be refreshed and the bigger life maintained.

The only reason the smash is bad for you is because you fear what the owner will say or think about you and you don't like being blamed or feeling guilty; you don't like the Mars element in your life. So it is not really bad for you except in your imagination.

In order to fear what the owner will say, or feel uncomfortable, you have to separate that which is life from your life. This can only be done in imagination.

Worry exists only in relation to you, the individual.

You can observe that whatever gives you the greatest pleasure will give you the greatest pain.

Do you see the stupidity of being surprised when life hits you?

To dodge the Mars element, which is life, you will have to die. Only death can save you, but you, the robot mind, regard the inescapable fact of death as the worst blow of life.

To wake up, to see yourself and all things as they are and not as you imagine them to be, you need a shock. There has to be something to keep disturbing you.

In the beginning you will find it impossible to stay conscious for longer than a second or two at a time. It is a tremendous effort to consciously observe yourself as you see the truth or the fact. The drag of unconscious sleep will overtake you just as ordinary sleep pulls at the lids and overtakes the exhausted man. But the Mars element in life will never let you down. It will shock you every time.

Whenever Mars strikes, say to yourself 'Mars!' and observe your reaction. If you just cry 'Mars!' and do not look at yourself reacting to the event you are wasting your time. If you do not see what responds at the moment of challenge, how can you know what you are?

In the beginning you will have to rely on Mars to wake you up, but if you can remember to observe yourself when Mars is not hitting you then that is very good. But you must never condemn, approve or judge your reaction. It is vitally important that you just observe.

You will find you cannot live with a fool once you see that he or she is a fool.

Unconscious people separate the Mars element from their lives by judging it as bad in relation to them. This creates conflict or friction — the judgment that it should not have happened to them against the fact of life that it did happen. The conflict or friction between what is and man's idea of what should be generates emotion, and this emotion is the energy that powers temper.

Say the same Mars situation happens to two men. One is unmoved inwardly, therefore conscious of all about him and able to take any intelligent action that might be needed. The other is a raging machine, quite unconscious because he can have only one thought at a time and his mind is aflame with exploding or simmering emotion. He is incapable of intelligent action and himself becomes a potential instrument of the Mars element.

The Mars element is pain and there is no mystery about pain, mental or physical: its purpose is to drive you towards awareness, to wake you up. If you see this, pain has a purpose, otherwise you suffer for nothing.

the immortal moment

THE STATE OF AWARENESS is the state in which you see things as they are: the precious facility that life has given man to escape the mastery of the robot. It is the habit of the mind to destroy the state of awareness as quickly as possible. It does this by judging, for judging is thinking.

If you want to see what is inside a room, you open the door and look in. To see everything exactly as it is you have to be in a state of awareness, in the mental attitude of listening, and this state is possible only when you are not thinking. You can only see things as they are when you do not think.

All your opinions, dislikes and most of your likes come out of memory. They are the result of some personal experience in the past or have been gained through reading, hearing, being influenced or conditioned. What you have experienced is all past. You cannot know what you have not experienced.

It is an inescapable fact that only the moment, now, exists in relation to you. Every moment is new. If you look at what is new through the screen of the past (your opinions) it is no longer new.

If you say you do not like the type of table in the room there are two possibilities. One is that it resembles a table you have seen in the past and stored as an unpleasant image in your memory. The second is that it is in some way new in your experience. It is the habit of the robot mind to reject the new. The mind hates change and you will always resist the new if it conflicts with your opinions, especially with what you imagine your interests to be.

Quite often you find that the new leaves you rather indifferent and it is difficult to decide whether you like it or not. You find this embarrassing at times because you cannot form an opinion, and everyone is expected by the intelligent robot mind to have an opinion. But after your mind gets used to the sight of the new, such as the design of a new car or a new look in clothes, you will probably find yourself saying you like it; or you will make up or steal an opinion.

Before introducing a new look experienced designers and manufacturers condition the public robot mind by publishing photographs and impressions as widely as possible. And politicians seldom introduce the new without first conditioning the public mind through a leaked newspaper or magazine story.

So if you say you do not like the type of table in the room your opinion is based either on the past or on the mechanical habit of the mind. Neither is an intelligent state. Dislike is the robot's judgment and a negative interpretation of the natural state of preference.

Preference, being the natural state, does not require thinking. That is why you like things without knowing why. What you mean when you say you do not like the table is that you would not choose it for yourself; you would prefer another. But it is not your moment to choose: you are judging someone else's moment, their preference. By doing that you divide yourself from them; and division is disharmony. When it's your moment to choose, just choose the one you prefer without disliking the ones you pass over. In that moment you are aware; and your choice is choiceless.

There is only one thing in your life you can be sure of. That one thing is this moment, now. The last moment has gone forever. The next moment has not come.

You can become fully conscious only when you are living in the moment. To begin to live in the moment you have to know it exists and understand it. To understand it you have to observe it in relation to yourself and in relation to life. When you understand it, when you become conscious, you will see it is all that exists. To see this is to glimpse reality.

Everything that happens to you — the good, the bad and the indifferent — happens in the moment. It is the mind's interpretation of the moment through an old impression that keeps you asleep. The moment occurs in your experience as a happening which is the fact. In the next moment your mind re-acts through a stored impression by responding to the happening as thought. You are then living in the past, hanging on to a moment that has gone. The moment, the new in life, is passing every moment, but by clinging to an old moment as an impression of this moment your mind keeps you unconscious of the only thing that exists for you.

The secret is that the moment is perfect. Thinking is the imperfection and is unnecessary. The more you observe life in relation to yourself the more you will see the fact that you are hardly ever correct when you think about something in the future. The future exists only in imagination; and that is why, no matter how hard you try to imagine it, you will not be able to predict the future with total certainty.

When you think about the future you invariably become

gloomy, doubtful, angry or fearful. You use your emotional impression-memory which leads to confusion, worry and wishful thinking.

Irritation at having to do something in the future is the jarring vibration of having put the moment out of place: you mistake the disharmony you feel now for trouble in the imagined future. The strange fact is that nothing is tedious or unpleasant at the moment of doing it, unless you think.

But how do you plan for the future if you do not think? You make plans by looking, not thinking. You use factual memory, not impression-memory. You plan by looking at the relevant facts of your experience and the looking itself reveals everything you need to know, moment to moment.

For example, to remember the things you own all you have to do is direct your attention onto them and then, without thinking, up they come, one by one. You cannot remember all you own at the same moment. The process is to ask yourself 'What do I own?' Your mind is temporarily stilled and up out of memory comes one object followed by another and another until the line runs out.

When making plans, you obtain any missing facts by taking action; then you look again. Once you have made a decision, or you find you cannot proceed any further, you drop the subject from your consciousness; there is no thinking or worrying. You just stay aware and look again from time to time to see if there's been any change in the situation.

Only one conscious action can exist at any one moment for any one individual. It is impossible for life to make two conscious demands of you at once. If it appears that there are two, one will be in your imagination — your impression of what you should be doing.

The moment is your only duty.

Your duty at any time in your life is to do what you have to do from moment to moment. What you have to do is what you cannot avoid doing. What you cannot avoid doing is what you do.

Life is not interested in the reasons that your mind produces for doing what you do. The reasons might or might not be correct, but the fact is always correct; and the fact is that you do it. It is the moment that is perfect and not the anticipation of it.

You do thoughtless, stupid, cruel, dishonest things. And afterwards either you or someone else labels the action in words; and mentally you suffer. You ask yourself, 'How could I have done such a thing?' But the fact is you did it. It is only because you are a machine that you suffer; and the purpose of suffering is to wake you up.

The moment is God's will.

Life reveals itself only to the conscious. Sometimes you will find yourself facing the Mars element, which is always from your point of view the apparent conflict of two moments, but what appears as disharmony to you is not disharmony in life. The disharmony is in the robot mind's desire to control life to suit its individual interests — an impossibility; but you keep trying.

We can rarely see things from the point of view of another person because we look at the facts through the screen of an impression or an interest which distorts our view; and then there are accusations, quarrels and misunderstanding.

You will become more conscious if you use the moment of being rebuked or blamed to observe your reaction. You will observe yourself making an excuse, giving a reason. You will make the excuse because you do not like being blamed.

Man always trots out an excuse. If the evidence is overwhelming and you can offer no explanation, you quickly find someone to tell your story to, with such wrong emphasis and lies that the listener will have to agree that your action was justified.

Each moment provides a challenge to you to become conscious. All things and all possibilities exist in the creation. You might meet someone; there might be a rain-storm, sudden pain, a letter, you might lose something — this is the world of the moment. No one can ever know what it will throw up because no one can ever know all it contains. The game is to be waiting, and aware.

TWO

MAN IS NOT AS COMPLEX AS HE OFTEN THINKS HE is (with a glimmering of satisfaction). He is complex in the sense that a tin of worms is complex. To the observer it is just a tin of worms. What the tin of worms is doing might be complex to the worms but the observer can tell without looking that they are wriggling and squiggling, like a tin of worms.

the man-machine

A MACHINE ALWAYS functions in a predetermined way. You can predict exactly what a machine will do if you have sufficient knowledge of it. A machine cannot go beyond the limitations of its design. It can stop, or run inefficiently, but it cannot of itself change the pattern of its function.

Trees and plants have different appearances but they all use the same mechanical process and their performance can be predicted. We can predict that they will absorb sustenance through a root system, form branches and produce leaves, flowers or fruit.

The cow-machine will give milk if it is fed and if mated will produce young in a certain time. It will run away from an outside cause of pain and attack you if you threaten its young. The dog-machine, or the elephant-machine, will function similarly, with slight variations. The water-machine, the light-machine, the sound-machine, the sun-machine, the moon-machine, the earth-machine: the performance of every machine can be predicted, according to our knowledge of it and making allowances for the Mars element.

Man is a machine whose direction can easily be predicted. He (she) will always devote his life to the desire for money, power and prestige. If he possesses any of these things and then loses them he is unhappy. And if he thinks he is going to lose any of them he worries. Whenever his desires are fulfilled he is happy, but only while he is thinking about or experiencing the fulfilment. Otherwise he is discontent and restless because of the non-fulfilment of other desires.

Predictably, like all animal and insect machines, he (and especially she) will protect the young even to death, imagining that man's love is above that of all the other animal and insect machines (which do the same thing, without the act of will that man says motivates him). The man-machine always gives preference to his own young over another's, and says that's natural, not understanding that what is natural is mechanical.

The man-machine imagines he possesses dignity. He goes to the most undignified lengths to prove it, being unable to understand that what possesses dignity does not need to prove it, and cannot lose it.

The man-machine will crucify any conscious man who tries to help him; and convert his wisdom into an empty, mechanical dogma that suits his own understanding. He will espouse a code of ethical behaviour based on the teaching of a man who was not a machine, and observe none of it — because a machine cannot change its function or understand what is true.

The man-machine fears death because a machine cannot see beyond its own destruction. He will also mourn the death of others; but only those to whom he is attached — as though their death were some unexpected event in life.

The man-machine imagines attachment to be love; and is baffled by the exhortation: 'Love one another.' The young, being made into machines by example and training, ask 'How can everyone love one another?' — for they have seen that no one does it, and know it to be impossible in themselves. But they will go on being mechanised by the imaginative answers and excuses of their elders.

Mechanical man is the composite image projected by life as it shines like a brilliant white light through three separate 'screens'.

The first screen is different for every individual. It is composed of the individual's experience of facts and impressions formed since birth. As every individual life is different, so the total experience of every individual is different and keeps changing with the accumulation of new impressions.

The second screen is not individual and nothing about it changes. It is the desire for power, a mechanical motivator designed to maintain man's activity through the desire for possessions and everything that goes with power.

The third screen changes every moment and consists of all things, states and possibilities existing in creation. Its moment-to-moment movement provides the interaction called 'time'.

The light passing through the screens blends the image of the individual with the mechanical desire for power and the endless opportunity to indulge it; every experience, impression and fact is converted into an expression of insatiable desire.

One of the greatest steps in self-discovery is to see that you are a machine.

Only the few who have real knowledge will admit to being machines. If you tell most people that they are a machine and that nearly everything, if not everything, they do is a mechanical reaction to influences outside their control they will probably say you are mad.

consciousness

YOU ARE WHAT you believe you are. You live, enjoy life and suffer according to that belief. But you probably cannot say what you believe you are. You can only say what you imagine you believe you are.

The truth, as always, lies in the source of all truth — life. What you believe, you live; or you do not believe it. Your beliefs can never be separated from your daily life and what you parade as your belief in discussion and argument is what you imagine you believe.

In the first instance, man believes he is his body and his identification with it actually dictates his life and destiny. But if you are only your body, then Christ, Buddha, Abraham and all the prophets were fools. And if you are not your body, what are you?

Your body is yours. Pinch it and it hurts. Pinch someone else and you feel no pain. But that does not necessarily mean your body is you. It could be an expression of you as the note is the expression of the bell. When the note has died, the bell still is. So your body is yours, but not necessarily you.

What drives you on? What makes you strive so hard? Why do you keep going when you are already under sentence of death?

The desire to exist.

If there is no desire to eat or breathe the body rots and vanishes. Remove desire and the body does not exist. So the body exists because of desire. But whose desire?

When you are asleep you are unconscious; you are absent. You exist only because you wake up and regain consciousness. While you are asleep and absent the body must be breathing because it is alive when you wake up. It is not your desire that makes the body breathe. Even while you are awake it is not your desire that keeps it breathing. Only when the breathing is impaired do you appear and do something about it. So the desire to breathe is not yours, but the body's.

The desire to eat is the body's too. You do not decide you are hungry. You first become aware of the sensation of discomfort in the body and then realise you are hungry. In the same way you feel well or sick, hot or cold. You do not decide any of these things. You always appear after the sensation and then decide what action to take. So it cannot be the truth that you are your body.

The terms 'unconscious' or 'subconscious' (as applied to our own minds) have no place in the science of self-discovery, except to spur us on. They only mean there is something about ourselves we do not know, and that is intolerable, for what is unknown might contain our freedom or immortality.

No one has ever discovered an unconscious mind in him or herself; what is discovered is unconsciousness as lack of self-knowledge. If you become conscious of the unconscious mind it is no longer unconscious. If you are unconscious of it, it's not you. Anything in-between is a partly observed fact or a theory.

There is obviously something determining your actions, the source of your desires and motivation. If you do not know what it is, and it is obviously not the 'you' that you imagine or believe yourself to be, it must be the 'real you' undiscovered. To label that 'the unconscious mind' is just another way of saying you are not all there. The term is usually an excuse for ignorance, used to account for something which in this living moment you are not experiencing.

If you want to study plant-life you must study plants. If you want to study the mind you have only one mind on which to work — your own. You cannot study someone else's mind as you can study a plant. You only imagine you can. No matter how hard you look you will not find another mind. You will only find another body.

The actions of your own mind can be observed in your body, but to study a 'mind' outside your own you will have to use your mind's impression of your body's impression of another body's impression of a mind. This is the unacceptable basis of every psychology that studies other minds.

Everything has consciousness because everything has knowledge. Where there is no knowledge there is no thing. Unless there is a knower (consciousness) there is no knowing and no knowledge.

To exist, a thing must first possess the knowledge to function as itself. If consciousness has only the knowledge of a worm it appears as a worm; if it has the knowledge of a dog, as a dog. While it has only the knowledge of a worm it will always behave like a worm. As consciousness knows, so it appears and behaves.

The study of the behaviour of a thing is the study of its knowledge. If we can find out what it knows we can predict its behaviour, which is exactly what the scientist does.

Man is the only thing capable of fully knowing its own knowledge or function. To know your function is to know yourself. Men and women seldom know themselves, but like all things they have degrees of self-knowledge; the degree is the knowledge which appears as function or behaviour.

Now we can see why man lives what he believes. He functions according to his knowledge of himself. If he does not know his knowledge or function he is not conscious and does not know himself.

If you do not know what you know it means you are not conscious.

To be conscious is to be consciousness: the knower, the supporter of all knowledge. Knowledge varies but consciousness cannot.

Consciousness, the knower in you, cannot be known, although it can be experienced. You can experience consciousness now by experiencing the fact that you exist. The difference between this and any other experience is that it is done independently of any state or thing. It is the only completely independent action man is capable of.

In this brief moment you will notice that you do not have to know anything. You do not even have to know you exist. You just are; or as you would say yourself, 'I am'.

You cannot hold that state because you start to think; not about anything in particular, but your mind runs off on an association prompted from outside by one of your senses. You think: you become that thought. And consciousness, or the state of pure awareness, is lost.

It is the way of things in this creation that every condition is the opposite of another. There is hot and cold, high and low, birth and death, pure and impure, gross and refined and so on. The movement of life, where it can be distinguished, always seems to be from the gross to the refined, from the impure to the pure. This eternal, seldom comprehended progression is what man knows as hope.

Knowledge follows this law. At one end it is gross, at the other refined. The lower end, in relation to existence, might be the knowledge possessed by a stone. In relation to man, the lower end might be the knowledge of a brute, the higher end the knowledge of a Christ or Buddha.

The highest knowledge man can possess is that which is true in his own experience. If his experience is limited, so is his knowledge and he behaves accordingly. A brute of a man cannot have had the same experience as a Buddha. But a Buddha must have had the same experience as a brute or there is no progression. The highest knowledge must be the most reliable too, or the law breaks down.

If someone tells you it is raining, and you look around and see it is not, you say it is not. It doesn't matter what authority the person has; you cannot be convinced otherwise because in your own experience at that moment you know the fact. You know it in the same way as you know you exist, and that is the supreme certainty of all experience.

The faculty you have used is logic. You have started with the first fact; your experience now. Logic always deals with first thing first. You might then say that you know it is not raining because when it rains you get wet and now you are dry. When you start to use the facts of your past experience, you start to use the faculty of reason. As reason moves further away from the living moment into more remote experience it becomes imagination, and the likelihood of error is increased enormously. Reason links man with factual memory. Imagination links him with impression-memory.

To know something in your own experience, just as you know you exist, does not require imagination. All you have to do is observe. You need no outside knowledge, no techniques, no talents as the world applauds them, no authority, no university degree, no books, no assistance. It is the simple, beautiful experience of aloneness (the opposite of loneliness).

The fact is always simple. The difficulty is in seeing it through the mind which always takes the imaginative way — until it is stilled. The mind knows it is the master in imagination and the slave of the fact. It will fight you all the way to self-knowledge. And why not? It is the only enemy.

Your memory is filled with uncountable experiences, a teeming jumble of unconnected matters right back to childhood. Yet when something comes up for discussion only the absolutely relevant details present themselves to consciousness and you express them.

You meet a person you have not seen for twenty years. In the second it takes to shake his hand you recall his name and most of the things you know about him and experienced together. This surely is a miracle. (Perhaps we have never observed it as such because we are always too busy looking for the miraculous.)

This miracle is the unifying principle of individual experience in this life. You have probably heard it called 'the ego'.

A 'principle' is a fundamental element that can be demonstrated but not defined. 'Unifying' means reducing to unity; which in terms of time means having continuity.

This principle unifies all your individual experience of life into the one amazing, intelligible, continuous expression which is you.

desire

WE HAVE SEEN that hunger and breathing are desires of the body. It is obvious from man's behaviour that he identifies himself with them because he has never bothered to observe their origin. There are other desires that are not of the body, but again man seldom pauses to observe these desires in himself.

For us who are observers of ourselves there can never be a hidden desire or hidden motivation. If we are always observing ourselves nothing hidden can come in without being spotted, and nothing hidden can get done, because we (the master) are always there.

If you want to do anything there has to be a desire. As soon as the desire arises in your consciousness it exists and you can see it; you can observe it for yourself — because then it is yourself.

Motivation is always the action of a desire and desire always produces its own energy for its fulfilment. The energy is produced through conflict; and conflict is produced by wanting to change what is. You can desire to go to the cinema but the desire-energy-action does not begin until the moment you desire to change what is, to change now. What is only exists now. Tomorrow is what may be. Yesterday is what was.

The first desire is for self-preservation.

You touch a hot iron. You withdraw your hand instantly; there is no thought or decision in the reaction. The body's desire is to protect itself so it withdraws from the abnormal heat which would otherwise injure or destroy it. It is the same with abnormal cold. When the hand sticks to something abnormally cold like the bottom of a refrigerator tray the mind is not sure at first whether the sensation is the burning of heat or cold. Both sensations are the same to the body. All it does is withdraw swiftly from whatever would destroy it. Desire for self-preservation is the motivator and the body performs without your assistance, without your thought or desire.

An example of interference with the body's desire: if you try to use thinking to regulate your breath it becomes irregular.

When the body smells toxic fumes in the air it tries to escape. Without a sense of smell it might be destroyed. In the same way, all the senses are a defence system — for self-preservation. The animals act in the same way; although unlike man they do not try to interfere with the system by thinking.

It is man's habit to see things in relation to his interests. If when you see a snake you perceive it only in relation to your self-preservation you will fail to see it as it is. You will fail to see the superb artistry of its skin pattern, the cold yet vibrant lustre, the wonder of its coiling movements, the brightness of its eyes, the nervous movement of its fine forked tongue. A snake is a thing of beauty if you look at it in relation to itself; (once you have satisfied the desire for self-preservation, of course).

Beauty is not an 'interest'; beauty is.

You are off to a business appointment. You take a short cut through the park. Your interest at the moment is in the appointment, so you see the trees and flowers only in relation to the appointment and are careful not to walk into the trees or trip over the bushes and flowers. You miss the beauty.

Beauty is in all created things if you can put aside your interests and see things as they are. How else do you think you see beauty, when you do — on those few occasions in your busy thought-full day?

Beauty is, despite you.

A tree will send its roots very deep, even under a road if necessary, to find food or sustenance. It has the desire for food and because of that it lives or is. If there is waste oil in the ground, the roots will avoid the place. If you keep chopping at a root it will grow in another direction. When you make a cut in a tree the sap congeals protectively around the wound, like blood.

From this you can see that the tree combines elementary states of the senses of smell, taste and touch-feeling. From the facts in our experience, we can say that the senses of smell, taste and touch-feeling are primarily associated with the desire of any organism, body or plant, to preserve itself.

Beyond the desire for preservation of the self, the organism or the species is the desire for power. Apparently trees do not see or hear, but animals do. The senses of seeing and hearing are the beginning of the desire for power and because animals have those senses there is a natural movement among them towards leadership, or dominance by the fittest.

This is where you come in, where man begins. The desire for power, for power's sake, is the beginning of mechanical man, the robot.

power

YOU ARE an expression of the desire for power. You devote your life to this desire. All your ambitions, all your strivings, are directed at satisfying it. When you imagine you achieve it you are happy; when you fail you are unhappy.

The body does not desire power. It does not want company. It only wants to be at ease, and ease includes exercise (when the body desires it). It needs water, food, air and a few other simple things to keep it at ease. If it itches, it scratches itself without any decision by you, even while you are asleep.

So it is not the body that desires power, but you. If you doubt that the pursuit of power occupies almost all of your life you must ask yourself what causes you the greatest worry and anguish.

The loss of a loved one can cause anguish but it will not interfere for long with the pursuit of power.

You will find the greatest cause is the anticipated loss of power as position, possessions, prestige and permanence; in other words, the loss of your power as an individual, which is death.

To enjoy power you have to see it exist in relation to yourself, the powerful, and someone else, the powerless or the impressed.

Your desire for power is partly fulfilled when someone praises you, honours you, obeys you, serves you, works for you, quotes you, borrows from you or listens to you.

You are also more powerful than another in your imagination when you can tell him something he does not know; or when you are first to break the news; or when you discuss in someone's absence their failings or excesses, especially in relation to your own morality and respectability.

Your motives for pursuing power are secondary to the pursuit; and they are imaginary. The pursuit is the fact; your motives are the excuses for the unending pursuit you cannot explain. The pursuit never varies but the motives, the reasons, the excuses are endless.

In a man's youth the motive, applauded by all, is the desire to meet the challenge, to pursue fame and fortune. When he gets responsibilities he pursues exactly the same things, only now the motive is called duty. From time to time there's an exciting challenge and he forgets his excuses or motives, pursuing success or power with zest; but always the tendency inside him is to pull back. A sort of weariness begins to show through, and this has to be quickly covered up.

In middle age the motive becomes security, or something like it. In old age, when the pursuit is old and has lost its vigour (but not its virulence), there are more frequent moments when man asks himself, 'What was it all about? What did I gain?' But by then it is too late, for soon anything gained will be taken in death.

It is no use having a fortune in gold if you are alone on a desert island. Gold or money is only valuable for what it will buy, which includes respect. If you had inherited an island teeming with people and wealth but were born deaf and blind you would get no elation from power, no feeling of success. You have to see your possessions or the power-producing effect of them. You have to see or hear the power of your authority.

The senses of seeing and hearing mark the beginning of what we term intelligence, which in man includes the faculties of reason and imagination. Without the senses of seeing and hearing imagination is almost totally absent, and without imagination there is no desire for power. For you can only desire what you can imagine.

fear

FEAR EXISTS ONLY in imagination.

The forces of imagination are so powerful that it is difficult for man to overcome fear (or the falseness of imagination). He tries using his reason, but few individuals ever succeed. Reason is a babe against the giant of imagination that keeps the poor, shuffling, robot world in chains.

Both imagination and reason are activities of the ego, the unifying principle of your experience in this life. The imaginative aspect of the ego is that every desire is pursued with the feeling, the conviction, that you are permanent — that 'it cannot happen to me'. But it does happen to you. It will happen to you.

There is no more obvious fact than death; but death seems to make no difference.

You imagine from moment to moment that you are permanent; and so identify yourself with that desire. But it is the desire that is permanent, not you.

When you are forced to look at death in relation to yourself, you fear it. When the surgeon looks at death in relation to a body on the operating table, he doesn't feel this fear. But he feels it when forced to face the fact of his own death.

Yet it is not death you fear, because you cannot fear what you do not know and you do not know what death comprises. You fear death because you know in your own experience that it will take away all your power, position, prestige, possessions — everything you imagine you are.

Fear is not a fact. It is an assumption.

Fear is your constant companion and merciless whip. The most pressing, ever-present fear is the fear of what people will say. You are afraid when you think you will lose your life, power or possessions. But you are not afraid in the moments of losing them.

You are always in fear, thinking, imagining, until the moment of action.

No one ever knows fear when they are not thinking; when they are aware.

A soldier's fear of going into combat may be greater than the fear of what his comrades would say if he held back. The army knows from experience that something like that can happen to a man with time to think, so training and discipline are aimed at making him obey instantly, without thought.

The body does not know fear, only the desire for self-preservation at the moment of threat, and then it acts within its limited capabilities. The ego, the unifying principle, protects the body in the moment of danger. But the problem is that in monitoring your senses you use your memory, imagination and reason to protect your body before the moment of danger occurs. As soon as the chattering chimpanzee of a mind sees or hears something it plunges into a jungle of associated ideas that are limitless in number in your memory. If you have one matter causing you concern, the mind will use every association to bring you back to it. It will suggest unending possibilities, most of them unfavourable or bad for you, because you are concerned or upset and expecting the worst. This is the ceaseless agony of worry.

If your desire for power, position, possessions and permanence disappeared your body would not die. All that dies is your fear.

faith

FAITH IS KNOWLEDGE. The reason people think it is something else is because they are superficial and live on the sandbank of themselves. And if they ever pause to peer into the deep crystal water around them they rarely penetrate beyond the dancing illusion of the sunlight on the surface.

You use faith all the time. It is your faith in the world that gets you through each busy day. But the trouble with worldly faith is that it is subject to error and the Mars element.

Real faith is knowledge of yourself.

'Have faith,' the preachers cry. You might as well cry 'Be hungry' to someone with a full stomach, or 'Be happy' to those whose hearts are heavy with sorrow.

Have faith?

'But I do not have faith,' a man may say to himself, as his puzzled child asks 'What is it? How do I do it?'

No one can explain faith except to say 'Trust me,' or quote the Bible; though if the truth were being lived, the words would not be quoted.

The fact is you cannot tell anyone to have faith.

You may say you do not have faith in God, Jesus Christ, or any other deity; but that is only rejection of the concepts that have been presented to you. Not to have faith means that the concepts of other minds are unacceptable. And so they should be. You cannot learn truth; you have to discover it in experience. Your non-faith or agnosticism is only the rejection of canned ideas.

All knowledge, all faith, is within you now, at this moment. That is why I have said you must not believe me. If you go inside yourself and know yourself through observation and awareness, you will know the truth of this and the truth will set you free of doubt.

You cannot be told any wisdom, any truth, that is not already waiting to be discovered just below the surface of what you call your conscious mind. A word of truth, an illustration of truth, can bring the dormant knowledge to the surface.

People can recite words of great wisdom with drama and never understand them, for the words have to match what they have discovered within.

The only test of what you know or believe is what you live by acting on. Anything else is imagination.

The world is full of 'I believers' and they really believe they believe.

Professional 'I believers' (politicians, broadcasters, newspaper pundits) know they are liars and poseurs. But what about the others?

If you pin an 'I believer' with an inquiry to discover whether he lives his belief, and he does not, he will equivocate, make excuses and lie; or if trapped he will indignantly declare 'I know what I believe!'

You have two honesties. The one you believe in and the one you live. You cannot adhere to the code you profess because your honesty changes with nearly every challenge. But because you are unconscious of this fact you excuse your inconstancy with the explanation that 'it was justified in the circumstances' — another expression of dishonesty.

There is no truth for the man-machine in a code that says 'You shall not kill. You shall not cheat. You shall not lie' — beautiful as that might sound. A moral faith is a static thing in a world of ever-moving desires. It is a denial of the fact of man's life.

'You shall not lie' — but you lie to hide the person you really are so that you will be liked or respected, or to give yourself the appearance of having more power or prestige than in fact you have; and also to give yourself the appearance of being more honest than you are. If a stranger came up to you and told you that you are a liar, that you cheat, deceive, hold bad will, are unkind and cruel and cannot control your passions, you would probably defend yourself vigorously. If he kept probing, you would probably lie some more and make excuses — all because you profess a code of honesty you do not live. Because everyone does it, everyone expects it. Eventually the lie becomes the way of life.

There is a permanent unchanging honesty, but you cannot know it until you rise above the man-machine that does not live what it professes to believe.

THREE

A BILLION MEN AND WOMEN BEFORE YOU PAUSED briefly in their burrowing in the past and sighed with an intensity beyond knowing:

'Where am I going? . . . What's it all about?'

But they received no answer.

Before you can escape from your burrow you must know you are trapped.

Then there's a chance.

beyond reason

WHAT REMAINS WHEN fear and desire have gone? Only you can find out. At the same time you will find out whether Christ, Buddha and all the prophets were fools.

If God exists, God can be experienced; but only by you. All the biblical prophets could swear on a stack of bibles that God exists, but you would be no closer to experiencing God.

If you have already found God through worship in a church or temple, through ritual and ceremony, through the teachings of a religious order, then that is good. But if you do not know that God exists, and you have a yearning you cannot explain, let us try to discover the truth together.

We know we exist because at any moment we can experience it. If anyone tells you they have seen a ghost, no matter how much you want to believe in the existence of ghosts you will not really accept it as a fact until you see a ghost with your own eyes — until you experience it.

The other way we accept things is by reason, the power to assemble facts in coherent form. We live our lives in reasonable acceptance that the mail will come, that the train will arrive, and that we will be alive tomorrow to carry out today's plan. But the mail or the train might not come. You might die in the night.

These things are unlikely, and reason will tell you so; but they do happen, every minute, somewhere.

Reasonable acceptance has to ignore the unlikely. As you know in your own experience, few people acknowledge the element of 'the unlikely' in the way they live; or the unexpected would not come to as a shock to so many.

Reasonable acceptance, our way of living, is imperfect. But God, if God exists, must be perfect and beyond reason.

Reason is a mighty faculty but it is still below the state of awareness, of pure experiencing, which is the state you are in when you know 'I exist' or 'I am'.

The fact is that unless you experience something for yourself it does not exist for you. Everything else exists in imagination first and then with reasonable acceptance. But imagination is unreliable and reasonable acceptance is imperfect.

If God exists you must have the experience of God in the moment; otherwise you are absent and God cannot exist for you.

To go beyond reason we have to climb up the ladder of reason and go to the top of it. This will not upset reason as it is interested only in assembling the facts, whatever they might be. Reason is an ever-loyal tool; imagination an ever-failing fool.

At the top of the ladder is awareness, or pure experience — the edge of yourself, and possibly the beginning of God.

Imagination is down below, left far behind. It ends where reason begins. To go to the edge of yourself you have to discard every image, every idea, everything you have ever read or been taught or heard about God.

To begin with, God is not good as you know 'good'. If you think

God is good, it is imagination — you are deluding yourself.

Perfection is obviously not the object in this world; if the Creator wanted a perfect world for us it would be perfect.

There can be no lasting happiness in imperfection so happiness is not the Creator's object — as you may have noticed.

In relation to the Creator, there can be no accidents within creation — or it is not the Creator's creation. God the Creator, if he exists, is creator of murder, suicide, disease, insanity, torture and devastation. God destroys the innocent child, the humble saint, the loving husband, the devoted son and daughter, the wise and good leader. At the same time God allows the murderer, the cruel, the merciless, the exploiter, all the so-called 'evil ones' to live. So God is not good as you know 'good'.

Whatever is good must surely depend upon the aim. But you do not know the Creator's aim, so you do not know what is good.

When you are fighting a war, anything that helps you win is good; any setback is bad. Do not 'men of God' on both sides ask God to bless creation by doing good for their own side? — 'good' which is bad for the other side. And at the same time they wish the bad upon their enemy, that also being good. Such is the stupidity of the imagination. While robot man imagines the object of his life to be separate from the object of all life, the entire creation, his 'good' and 'bad' must forever follow this crazy pattern of inconsistency.

From the Creator's standpoint what is good must be good for the entire creation; and every individual thing must exist to contribute towards the overall object, irrespective of its personal idea of good. What is, is best.

And if God does not exist, if there is no overall purpose and no overall good in relation to the entire creation, it doesn't matter anyway.

Many mystics have said, and it is true, that anything you see is not God. Anything you think is not God, neither are visions, lights, moving objects or anything else. Any sensation or feeling is not God. They are all the products of the creation or your imagination.

You may have visions and psychic experiences and you will be excited about them. You will think you are making progress; but it will be down the hill if you busy yourself with them. You will have taken a false trail made by the creation or imagination. If you experience the Creator you can be sure there will be no room for doubt.

Plenty of people and books will tell you about psychic experiences. The experiences do exist as part of the creation. If you want to talk about them you will never be short of listeners or advisers, but God is way beyond them and God is our object.

The Creator has to be experienced beyond the five senses and the only instrument that can experience in this way, for you, is yourself — in the state of thoughtless awareness in which you declare 'I am' and hold it.

In the beginning the entire creation seems to hinder, obstruct and try to keep you away from experiencing the Creator. It is the way of things that only the unrelenting, indomitable individual can escape and experience God. The curious masses always fail. Later on, all things help, not hinder, the valiant ones.

On the way to God you have to pass through beauty, pure beauty. If you do not pass through beauty it is not God that you find. Beauty stands at the gate of the kingdom of heaven. It is of the Creator, but not the Creator; and it is all-mighty.

Beauty is the only uncreated thing you can experience apart from God.

You experience beauty when you look at a sunset, the sea or the forest and an indescribable thing happens within your whole being for the briefest of moments. Then it is gone, and no matter how much or how long you continue to look at the beautiful thing, beauty does not return. You turn away and then without thinking you suddenly look again; and again beauty strikes your deepest note — and is gone again. But the beauty is not absent. Beauty is and always is. You are absent.

Why are you absent? What keeps you from this indescribable ecstasy, this love, this truth, this peace? It must always be there — because others experience it just as fleetingly, even while you do not.

Again your robot mind is the problem. It will not stay still and you cannot make it stay still. It is your master and it separates you from beauty and God. Beauty is experienced only from moment to moment. It cannot be held in memory and it cannot be willed.

You can only experience awareness, the highest state, from moment to moment — when there is no object, no reason, no action, no mind. So to experience beauty, love, truth and peace, or God, your mind has to be stilled.

Imagination is mostly desire without object or action, and without the intention to act. When you do act on imagination, it's on impulse and you nearly always fall flat on your face. You experience this mostly in personal relationships.

You spend most of your private life imagining — wishing, worrying and building on impressions. Imagination is where you build on what someone told you about someone, where you impute motives, infer insults, and where you speculate about what someone meant by the inflection of his voice.

You can be ninety per cent certain that when you use the words 'if' and 'should' you are about to enter imagination.

Planning is reason with an object and the intention to act.

When you make a plan, your reason presents you with the facts, although there is no action yet. You accept that within reason your intention or plan will be carried out. Go beyond reasonable acceptance and you drop into imagination.

This is the line between the intelligent and the unintelligent person in the world; between the sought-after man with his feet on the ground and the fool with impractical schemes who worries himself into ill-health and calls it 'nerves'.

Thinking is mistaking impressions for facts.

Reason does not need thinking. If you observe yourself making a plan you will notice that having fixed the object, the facts just keep coming, linking up into a chain of proposed action. But when you are using imagination, going beyond reasonable acceptance and building on impressions, you will notice you build outwards, away from yourself.

Worry has no object; you only imagine it has. The process is most dissatisfying and you know it is stupid, even while it is going on.

Awareness is experiencing from moment to moment.

The beginning of awareness is reason with object and action.

Reason acts quickly in awareness, a thousand times faster than thought, and you do not even notice it is operating. Driving a car is an example of this.

You are always in the state of awareness when you love what you are doing. You are aware all the time, for love keeps you awake and in union with the action. You are also creative in this state, although the state of awareness diminishes as you get used to the job and then you go back to sleep.

When you attain your object the moment of attainment

cannot be held. The moment is part of the creation, so it is in time and must die — as everything in the creation must die so that the next moment can be born.

The moment is the last created thing, in relation to you.

This state of awareness lasts as long as the action. When the action is over you begin thinking; and you are then out of the state of meditation, which is what awareness is.

There is a further state of awareness. For the purposes of description, this is reason with an object but without action. The object is the state itself: it disappears in experiencing the state.

You are in this state of awareness the moment you experience that you exist — that 'I am'.

This experience stops the mind momentarily. You draw all your faculties into yourself; you meditate on the moment and you experience 'I am'. But only for a moment. You are still in time, and still in the creation, so the moment of attainment must die. But in the moment of the experience there is no reason, no object, no action — just 'I am'.

This experience is at the edge of pure awareness. If you could hold the state, even the 'I am' would disappear. You would be in the silence on the edge of time; and for a split second at the apex of consciousness. Just beyond is where God, the timeless or the uncreated begins — beyond the moment, the last created thing.

When you start to enter this awareness you are only able to remain in the state long enough to experience 'I am'. You can repeat the experience but it will still last less than a moment and be gone. You cannot hold the state in the wandering, ever-desiring condition of your mind. If you think you can, look again . . . You're imagining it. You will see that although you are in a state of no apparent thought, you are not aware of your environment. It's like staring into space: you are not aware, you are absent and unconscious of your existence.

You can only get next to God through the effort of preparation. To experience the uncreated, the state of awareness will have to be held for several minutes. But if it can be held for minutes, it can be held for hours; and if it can be held for hours, it can be held continuously. You are then between time and the timeless — waiting for the unknown, which will come but cannot be willed.

You will then understand why a man once said 'I am in this world but not of it.' Here you can eventually realise not only 'I am' but 'I am God.'

will and desire

CAN YOU CHANGE your desire for money so that it is gone and never returns? Or your desire for power or prestige which you are pursuing so vigorously? You cannot. What would you change it to anyway? The desire to be honest all the time?

Of course you can say you do not want to change, meaning you do not desire to; which means you desire the desires you're already pursuing. You cannot change while you desire.

Your strongest desires dictate what you do. They are the key that winds you up like a toy rooster that struts around for a few minutes imagining it is doing what it wants; at the same time imagining it is being honest because it is obeying the mechanical law which is its very existence.

You may say that you do things you do not desire to do. But that is an example of imagination and lack of self-knowledge. While you desire to exist, you have to put up with all that is involved in that desire.

If you renounce anything, you renounce nothing. Renunciation is a reaction of desire and a part of the original desire itself. By renouncing something all you do is change the direction of your desiring and continue with the same drive as before.

You cannot change your desires; they change themselves

under the following circumstances — when they are fulfilled, no longer appear to offer satisfaction, or some alternative means of fulfilment has appeared; when you realise the desire is false or it causes so much pain that a desire to avoid it replaces the original desire.

The basic driving desire for power can never be fulfilled. But it can cease to exist when you experience most of what power stands for, and see with an indescribable realisation that it is nothing, that what you have always been chasing is just a road to nowhere.

A man falls overboard from a ship into a cold ocean and swims around all night before he is picked up. It is incredible how he was able to keep going. Will-power? No. Desire-power. His desire to survive was stronger than his desire to give up.

A businessman loses everything in a financial crash, begins again, working fourteen hours a day, seven days a week, and in three years rebuilds his business. Will-power? No. Desire-power. His desire to be a success or to possess money and power was stronger than his desire to be a good family man or husband or anything else.

A fat woman known for her gluttony goes on a diet and in three months reduces to trim proportions. Will-power? No. Desire-power. Her desire not to be fat was stronger than her desire for food.

There is nothing wrong with desire-power, for it is life itself. But desire-power is not will-power.

Desire-power is easily identified: you will always imagine that you stand to gain something by using it. The greater the desire-power, the greater the effort or sacrifice. But because desires vary with every individual, and because ways of achieving these desires also vary, one person may display tremendous desire-power where another does not.

You will notice that we do not use the expression will-power when a person saves another's life. We say he was brave or fearless. If he does it without thinking it is an act of love, but if he thinks before he acts it is because he imagines there is something in it for him, even if it is only that his desire not to be called a coward is stronger than his desire not to go to the rescue. A man who thinks never goes to certain death to save another. If he does, he thinks he will make it.

Man's development from a machine into a conscious man depends upon his discovering and understanding the principles of will-power and love. Understanding of will-power leads to understanding the principle of love.

Will is the power that overcomes desire.

Will-power is equilibrium, the absence of desire or reaction. Anything that is equalised is in balance, at rest.

Life is held together by will-power.

Desire can be said to manifest in all living things and to reach a peak of expression in man, but it utterly fails to affect the equilibrium of what is. Every single thing that desires dies, is inevitably annihilated. And life goes on, untouched and serene. Whatever it is that holds life together has obviously overcome desire.

The results of desire-power are tangible and enviable; but you will not be seen to gain anything desirable from applying will-power. There is nothing at all in it for the man-machine.

Will-power can be exercised only in yourself. It cannot be inflicted on anyone or anything outside; not even on your own body. If you try to do that you will be using desire-power.

Will-power is an energy; the finest and most combustible energy in the human organism and the first energy to be destroyed in anger and other emotional reactions.

You tap into will-power, and start overcoming desire, when you observe yourself getting angry or impatient and can smile, let go of the emotion and die to it, because you see its futility.

Will-power does not mean suppression, which is merely a reaction of desire.

Being able to use will-power depends first on your alertness in being present when the emotion is actually rising in you. Second, it depends on your ability to counterbalance the emotion by immediately understanding that you are identifying with your desire; that the emotion is imposing a false claim on you.

No desire is individual. Desire is the stamp of the herd, the unconscious mass. The desire of the body for food is the desire of all bodies, which means the desire itself is not individual. But you will insist on associating your individuality with pursuit of the common desire for power, possessions, position or prestige. Only the instant understanding of this false claim it is making on you as an individual can enable you to cut off from it and be free of it without frustration.

You can assume for the purpose of discovering will-power that virtually everyone you know except yourself is moving in an eternal mechanical circle and believes with a conviction as strong as life itself that it is the only practical way to live. You either go with them, or you go against them, but they will feel it. No will-power is needed to go with them, only desire-power, and not much of that. Anyone who falters will be dragged along.

Everyone has desire-power. But will-power is buried under

it. Until you have started to realise the pain and futility of living as desire, will-power remains hidden and involuntary. The first sign of it beginning to show through is when a person pauses, stands back for a few moments from identification with the busy world and sighs 'Where am I going? What's it all about?' If this occurs in the midst of sorrow caused by frustration, disappointment or loss, nothing is likely to come of it. But if it occurs at all sorts of times, especially in moments of success and gain, the person is ready. And the next sign is when you see that you are not free; and that you, and you alone, are to blame.

love and desire

WHY IS IT that you do not really love, and you know it?

Why is it that so often you have to pretend to love those you love?

Love is giving of yourself.

Your possessions are not of yourself so to give those is not love. Your house, food, money are not of yourself so to give those is not love. If you have lots of money you can give lots of things, but if you have no money you can give none. The homeless pauper must be able to love too.

When you give advice, that is of your experience. When you give your opinions that is of your pride. When you say 'I love you' that is of your breath. When you work for others, feed them, house them, educate them, you work for yourself first. When you give of your time you must take it from something else and taking can never come into giving.

You just give your love, you say?

No you do not. The hen and the sow do as much for their own. You have no love to give and that is why you know you do not love.

Yet you can love . . .

But only in the moment.

Love is ever-moving, like everything else, and yet it is constant.

Man imagines he contains love and makes a static thing of it, like honesty. Then he is shocked when he sees he does not love. This makes him lie to those he 'loves', and worse, to himself.

Man's love is desire. To desire is to want to receive. Man imagines his love is something he gives, but this cannot be.

When men and women love each other it is expressed as the desire to be together, to live together. Their desire gives them no peace until they are together. They imagine that as soon as they are together it will be the fulfilment of the desire. Despite their later denials they imagine that fulfilment will carry with it a continuing state of happiness or contentment. Otherwise they would not love or desire each other. But desire wants to receive and this means they are taking, not giving.

Both of them are receiving the beautiful feeling of love. But where is it coming from?

Love itself is giving.

Love is a power, a mighty principle that exists in its own right independent of any individual. Man changes, but the principle of love does not and cannot.

Love does not leave men and women. Men and women leave love.

Man's desire for his loved one is doomed to disappear in the very delight of its fulfilment. The desire to be together, the desire to know the other, to experience everything about the other, is the basis of man's and woman's love. But when you know everything about something, you contain it, are one with it and begin to lose interest in it. So to continue to desire another with the same freshness as when you first fell in love, the beloved has to have a quality of timelessness, of the unknowable.

Whenever you desire anything, you desire knowledge. This is because you cannot add anything to yourself except knowledge. It does not matter what you possess, you cannot add it to yourself. All you add is the knowledge that you possess it and can experience it or use it at any time. This knowledge is the fulfilment of the desire for an object.

Your body needs air. You desire the knowledge that the air is there. Once you have that knowledge the desire, for you, is fulfilled. Otherwise you would worry and try to organise a continual supply of air for the future.

You desire to read a book. You do not desire the book as an object, or if you do, you want only the knowledge that the book is in your possession so that you can experience it at any time. When your desire is fulfilled you do not read the book again — the knowledge is already yours and there is no desire.

You desire power. The only way you know your desire is being fulfilled is by seeing or hearing others obey you. If you were in a prison cell and kept sending out orders without knowing they were being obeyed, your desire for power would not be fulfilled and you would probably be called mad.

The fact of human love is that man or woman desires to live with the loved one so that he or she can absorb the other entirely, possess them by knowing everything about them. This desire contains its own destruction.

The period of fulfilment, of knowing each other, does not usually last very long; because there is not much to know and not much worth knowing in men and women unless they love God or the truth. Truth and God are depthless and timeless and those who love them develop the same qualities. But usually what you get to know is mostly personality; and personality is an act. You cannot act all the time. As each sees the truth of what the other is, the masks are left off more and more. The painted faces are brightly displayed for others to see; but there is little mystique between the former lovers. The partnership is mechanical and predictable.

To begin with, love is longing, the separation of a desire from its fulfilment — plus the brief period of fulfilment. Then it is sex, expectation, fear, compatibility, familiarity and habit. If the desires or interests of the two people are similar, their union usually results in a kind of oneness. If most desires can be fulfilled as a partnership reasonable peace remains; if not, there is conflict.

Love is all around you like the air and is the very breath of your being. But you cannot know it, feel its unfeeling touch, until you pause in your busy-ness, are still and poised and empty of your wanting and desiring.

When at rest the air is easily offended and will flee even from the fanning of a leaf, as love flees from the first thought. But when the air or love moves of its own accord it is a hurricane that drives all before it.

The understanding of love comes with the knowledge that you are nothing. The greatest purity is nothing or nothingness — no thinking, no desiring, no imagining. You are then one with the moment and the great movement of life so nothing can happen that is not right. Every moment is perfect and everything that happens is eternally just.

strife

THE ETERNAL LAW of magnetism is that opposite attracts opposite and like repels like. In the electrical circuit the flow is the same: connect positive to positive or negative to negative and nothing happens. Yet in the world of man, or the world of man's mind, like attracts like and opposites repel. How can there be two contradictory laws?

Man's world is the world of his mind. His mind is the source of his personality, ambition, like and dislike, good and bad. In everything man is either for or against. He says there are two sides to every question but what he says is not true: there can only be two sides if personal interests, which means selfish interests, are involved. Otherwise something is either true or false, or the facts available at the time are insufficient to allow a conclusion to be reached.

If two people want to establish whether an animal is a cow they look at it and say, 'Yes, this is a cow.' There are only the facts of what a cow is. There are no selfish interests or opinions (man's most treasured possessions). But if one of them says it's his cow and the other says it is not, there is a difference of opinion. They are now in the world of mind where like attracts like and opposites repel.

The Hindus will tell you the cow is sacred. That is their treasured opinion and there are several hundred million of them. You may disagree. It is a case of for and against, a matter of opinion; but not a matter of fact because no mind knows.

In the mind-world no one knows all the facts so there is little hope of complete agreement. In the mind-world treasured interests and beliefs are anyway more important than facts. So issues invariably polarise into two opposing sides of opinions and beliefs.

Men would rather talk than act, so the air and their ears are continually battered with opinions that are seldom backed up with any action other than the automatic expression of them.

But the fact is that both sides are always wrong. The argument in favour could not exist without the argument against. Remove the arguments and there is no dispute. What remains is the fact; and you cannot argue over a fact.

Factions arise from looking at the argument — instead of looking for the fact. When two factions go to war it is to prove nothing but the force of their respective arguments, while the fact of the matter is left ignored and undiscovered. By the time the factions have finished fighting, the fact they failed to see at the outset is not only still invisible but probably no longer apposite. Every fact has its moment and now the moment and the fact have moved on.

No disagreement can be resolved except by action. Nothing is ever resolved except by action. Then the side that has the stronger means of arguing (not necessarily the correct argument) becomes the fact, if it matters. When you have the power you have your way.

But what always happens in the end? Julius Caesar fought some mighty battles. So did Napoleon. Where are their empires now? In 1945 after five years of war and millions of dead, the Allies proved the most powerful. Then came the cold war. Communist opinion was that their system would be good for everyone; the West disagreed. The most powerful always decides.

Do you see a pattern?

Where have man's opinions been taking him since the beginning of history? Where are your opinions taking you?

Nowhere. Except towards useless conflict. There is nowhere else to go.

While you remain mechanical, all that life demands of you is that you keep busy doing nothing so that life's greater purpose (beyond your busy imagination) can be eternally served.

The eternal law, contrary to the law of man's mind, is that heat attracts cold and cold attracts heat, until a balance or equilibrium is reached. This balance in creation supports life on earth between the cold of the poles and the hottest place on earth. Similarly, light attracts dark and dark attracts light until a balance is reached. If there was no dark in the light we would be blinded; and if there was no light in the dark something equally damaging and incompatible would happen.

You will notice that this attraction of opposites, each tending to cancel the other out, is a process of de-creation; but that it always stops arbitrarily at the point of balance needed to support life. If it were allowed to continue past that point, the opposites would eventually unite like desire and its fulfilment — and the creation would disappear. Nothing would remain except the state that existed before the creation began.

The precise opposite to this process is man's self-centred creation, his world, in which like forces attract each other — like attracts like and hate attracts hate. Man's world is an attempt to create something within the creation itself. This is a clumsy sort of reverse process that is self-propagating instead of self-cancelling, divisive instead of unifying. If man has his way, the 'likes' and the 'hates' will continue to grow and spread until the whole world condenses into immovable blocks of intractable opinion.

But man does not have his way: war and fighting see to that. In man's self-centred, self-conscious world, war and strife are necessary equivalents of the violent function of nature in the natural world. They are life's way of breaking down the monoliths and providing the breathing space for them to breed again.

As nature through the law of opposites uses violence and destruction to preserve and replenish itself in perfect harmony, so the discordant man-made world depends on war and strife to preserve itself in perfect disharmony.

divide and die

THERE IS an eternal law that can guide man. It will never leave him in doubt about what he should do. It contains no room for extenuating circumstances, justifications or changing values of the kind that snarl up man-made and mind-made laws. It is a law that the innocent bewildered part of man can understand. Even though he may infringe it, he can see for himself at every turn of the way the unerring signpost of eternal justice.

The law is: Divide and die.

This law does not refer to physical division but to the mental fences we erect. We live in a narrow no-man's land of fences that divide us from the world on one side and our being on the other.

You are your being when you know the moment of love and experience the happiest, most ecstatic moments of your life — moments that do not come from fulfilling any desire you can name. It is your being that knows love. It is your being that knows beauty.

Your being is your self made conscious. Your non-conscious self is mechanical man with his robot mind. The robot cannot experience love or beauty. Nor can it know your being. But when the mind is still and innocent of desire it becomes transparent.

Then you become your being and you shine through the machine like a thousand suns. You feel divine. And you are.

Your being unites: your mind divides.
Division is death for your being and life for your mind.
Only by division does the individual robot grow.
Union is death to your mind and life to your being.
Union is immortality.

When you smile and mean it, in the moment of giving yourself your being reaches out and unites with the object of your smile. It might be two birds playing on a branch or an infant trying to stand up. In smiling you have added the object to your being; and yet you have given of yourself. You become bigger; and yet you have become smaller. It is your beautiful being that is bigger: your divisive thinking self is smaller. You don't suffer when you smile.

When you frown or scowl you divide yourself from the object or event. Instead of going out to it, you step back from it. Your beautiful being shrinks and you, your mind, the thinker, the judge, the divider, the individual robot, grow bigger. You have divided yourself from another and by the eternal law you must suffer. The immediate penalty for breaking the law is unhappiness — feelings of irritation, anger, hatred, envy and bitterness.

But this is an eternal law too. Its justice is felt in the eternal world as well as in time. While you go on breaking this great law you separate yourself from immortality; for it is your being that is immortal. Unless you are being your being you are not immortal.

To divide yourself from your being is living death. But that is how man lives — in a sort of death which he treasures as life.

Do you see the superb justice of this great law?

You do not really harm others with your scowl or curse. You harm yourself.

This law is for the individual alone, because only individuals can learn to be honest with themselves. All the world may say a man has done wrong, but if he knows his words or actions have not been divisive, he is free.

Only the individual can know if he or she has obeyed the law. And the knowledge is important only to the individual.

Your being knows only two states. One is the state of neutrality or rest; the other is beauty.

The harmony of beauty is in being. When you suddenly see something of beauty, and you like it immediately, without thinking, its beauty has struck the same note of beauty in your being.

There are no opposites in being; no liking or disliking. Neither beauty nor neutrality requires judgment. They are states, just as immersion in water is a state, and you do not have to judge or think to experience them.

Being either likes and loves (and in the absence of thought that is beauty); or being is neutral and life is spent in innocent indifference to most of the things around you.

Mind is busy all the time. It hates the state of neutrality, or being at rest without an interest to occupy it, because that threatens its mastery. When it encounters the state it rushes for a book or the television or someone to talk to.

Mind's desperate measures to fill every moment keep you from consciously being your immortal being. To consciously reach your being you have to resist the mind's constant demand for activity, and endure the restlessness, loneliness and discontent.

If you feel disharmony with a person or in a place, then go. There is no need to be divided. Unite yourself with another place or person.

If a man is foolish and you can show him (perhaps vigorously but always quietly) that he is foolish, then both of you will gain and most men will thank you. If you can't, leave him in indifference. But if you call him a fool and try to give him your opinion, he must in return give you his; then both of you will be right and both of your opinions will be wrong.

If you would do good, or want to help, be careful you do not intrude. If you would outspeed the moment and chase a 'good cause', be sure you are prepared to die for it. Otherwise you are intruding on yourself and dividing yourself from yourself. However good the cause may seem to be, if it is the way it appears to you that is inviting then the mind is inviting you to work for the cause. And so you will be working first and foremost for yourself. The need of anything is known only to being. If you are something's need you will be united with it as help. You will have no choice, nor want one.

If you ever have to kill make sure it is not you who pulls the trigger or pushes the button. Let the man-machine do that while you remain conscious, watching from your being in the state of equilibrium. If you do kill, only you will know whether you intruded. If you did not intrude, then the robot will have died a little with your victim. You are not special; you may have to kill. If the man-machine was not meant to kill there would be no killing.

You have two prides. The one you know is the one of your mind, your imagination. This pride you will vary or bury to satisfy a desire of the moment and resurrect when you imagine you are offended. But your true pride is of being and it will never let you sink below your essential dignity. This pride is beyond knowing, but not beyond observing. It is of the moment and its power is truth and innocence. It is the dignity of life itself and life will defend that dignity, killing you to preserve it if necessary. When this pride rules you will die for it — willingly, fearlessly, with a smile on your lips; not out of defiance, but out of compassion for those who would imagine they can separate you from your eternal dignity.

impersonal love

GREAT LOVE DESTROYS people because those who love personally and exclusively cannot contain love as it really is.

Only the stellar system is profound and total enough to illustrate the possibilities of the love of man and woman.

The universe, in fact, is life's symbol of their potential.

Love's destruction of a man or woman is the making of a star.

The making of a star is love incarnate; untouchable, unattainable except through the destruction it surely and lovingly works among those who love the earth — those who see the light but not the star.

The star is in the beholder.

Love that does not begin to glimpse its own beauty within the beholder is earthbound and deathbound. Love that does is also doomed, but in a different way; it has to go beyond the earth and its exclusive loving into the terrible aloneness of deep space. The journey is a self-consuming destruction of all the previous personal love that would endeavour to preserve the persons loved, with beautiful motive but untenable selfishness, denying them the inevitable destiny of becoming their own star.

So the love of my children becomes the love of any child; my mother, any mother; my people, any people; my love, all things; my life, all life. And each moment of love is dictated by where I am and what I do, for where I am is life.

Life's infinite appeal is its refusal to compromise with death, destruction or man's ideas of good and evil.

Because man cannot face the fact of life's infinite destruction, he fears.

Fear is anxious caring. Life does not care; and yet it cares beyond all caring for it destroys and rampages only so that the infinite play of life may continue.

Can man live like life?

Can he stop fearing, or anxiously caring?

Can he destroy his fears and ideas every moment as life destroys itself, and begin fresh and new every moment?

Can he cease to compromise, not with people, but with his fears of what people will say or think? For apart from fear of tomorrow, that is perhaps his most virulent fear.

Can he never again look back with sorrow or regret on what he has done? And so cease compromising with his imagination and excuses?

When man ceases to compromise with himself he finds caring turns to love.

A woman's perception is different to a man's, more intuitive; so her way is different.

Women have less habit in them than men. The grooves of habit do not run so deep. Their clinging is more superficial. They are more able to forego and forbear when their outer crust is penetrated.

They have more love in them than men; not the superficial love that in most women clings or even serves, but the unexpressed love that plays across the grooves of habit to diminish them. This is the terrible unpredictable love that draws, weakens and destroys man.

This love is the thing in woman that a man says he cannot understand. It is her forgetfulness, her flightiness, her unreliability, irresponsibility and caprice; all the elements that destroy her own habit and man's expectation. All searing, universal, impersonal love. When woman is made perfect, and she is all this love, she is uncontainable.

FOUR

MAN CANNOT KNOW THE TRUTH OF LIFE OR DEATH until he knows himself.

Man is desire, relationship, thinking, talking, action, trying, reaction, emotion, understanding, sleeping, dreaming, judgment, attitude, silence, response, listening, words, and perception.

When you see through these things in yourself they dissolve as obstacles to your perception of the magnificence that lies behind them.

ego *and* desire

DESIRE IS STRESS or strain. It is a tension between you and the thing or state you desire. As the thing does not feel this stress, the desiring is a one-way tension within you, an apparent reaching out towards the object or person.

When the person responds in the way desired, or the object is attained, the desire settles down into a relationship. A relationship is identifiable by the presence of an attitude in yourself which reacts in terms of 'mine'. Its impurity is clinging.

The strength of a relationship cannot be known until after it is broken. Then the original desire reappears, modified by experience. It continues to be modified by repetition of experience until eventually it vanishes. Unsuspected by the long-suffering desirer, its final stage is usually a shadow-existence of thinking and going back over the past, powered by nothing more than habit. Every habit is a track left by desire.

Desire itself can only be eliminated by desiring, and that always results one way or another in pain for the desirer. Living is just that: ceaseless desire eliminating and reforming itself by the pain and frustration of its own wanting.

When a desire has been reduced to the level of a habit or idea it can be dealt with and eliminated fairly quickly by observation — seeing it for what it is. In that moment you suddenly realise you are free of the relationship as a need or dependence 'of mine'.

This is the only freedom, at any level of existence.

The feeling of desire is a feeling of need, of the need to have or do something. The greater the feeling of need the more we think about the desired object. But the more we think about a thing the more we exclude ourselves from the experience of the rest of our life. As the desire becomes more intense it takes over more and more of our thinking and unless we can translate all the thinking into action (when thinking should cease) we begin to experience desire's peculiar discomfort or pain.

This feeling is the strain of desire in us. It is the result of self-contraction, the limitation of ourselves, the constriction of our being. It is a cry of anguish from our desireless will, whose power and freedom is the absence of desire.

There is no desire without thought. The more desires we have the more we think.

Most people think all the time, even when there is no apparent working of desire in them. This is thinking caused by the ego's desire to exist.

The ego's desire to exist supports an individual's personality. There are several distinct aspects to every personality, although the distinction between them is not clear-cut in ordinary circumstances.

All desires are really part of the ego's desire to exist. But as they each represent a need, they have specific objects and therefore follow specific thought-lines characteristic of the different aspects of the personality.

The personality-ego relationship might be illustrated by a leather football. The surface areas marked off by the stitching are the facets of the personality. The leather itself is the ego, the substance that supports all aspects of the personality and presents them on the outer surface, though not all can be seen at any one time. Of course the leather also has a thickness, and an inner surface which contains the space inside the ball, so in the same way the ego has distinct identities according to its function.

The ground of personality (the outer surface of the ball) is the response or reaction to specific external stimuli.

Personality always has the object of impressing itself on someone or something. It goes into the memory and selects only what it needs to serve its immediate interests. It puts back only what it believes will serve its interests in the future.

This selective reactivity is life to the personality.

The ground of ego (the inner surface of the ball) is the memory.

Unlike personality, ego has no selective interests. It is only interested in receiving knowledge — any knowledge at all, dirty jokes, pious prayers or the highest truth. The memory is a garbage tip for information. It is immaterial to the ego whether the data is true or false.

To the ego life consists of experiencing itself as a personality; receiving information; and experiencing what it already knows by thinking about it.

The ego's desire to exist is our desire to know. It is our most insatiable and powerful longing, stronger even than the body's desire for survival.

The ego collects information by aimless listening, watching, gossiping and reading. It experiences what it already knows through aimless day-dreaming and associative thinking. It has the emotional involvement of a cow chewing the cud — until it is denied information, and then in an uncontainable fury of desire it will directly enter the world as an inexplicable impulse.

At times the ego may not be actively gathering information, and the personality may be dormant. But the ego still insists on experiencing itself as memory. So it thinks: we think.

Any thought at all will satisfy the ego, for it is concerned only with experiencing. It is irrelevant to the ego whether the experience is thinking, dreaming, killing someone or serving tea.

The superficial personality (like the surface of the football) and the all-encompassing ego (the leather) receive their power and shape, flexibility and responsive tension, from the pressure of 'air' within.

The air is beyond the ego but where it meets the leather on the inside of the football a force is exerted. And this force acting on the ego is what is called 'the id'.

The id is a battery of energy, the powerhouse of the ego and the personality. It supplies energy for every reaction, including the reactive principle of the body itself, which keeps the heart beating and actuates the nervous-system.

The pressure of the id is constant. Although the force may appear to dissipate when the energy is spent in physical or emotional reactions, its constant original pressure supplies unlimited energy. What appears to dissipate is not the energy but its medium, the ego, which is subject to decay or death.

The id-entity is what we recognise as 'my consciousness'. When an individual becomes sufficiently conscious of himself as one whole entity, the ego and personality cease to have separate identities. Depending on the individual it may take months or years for this integrated consciousness, or 'super-ego', to become established in the body.

This integration of ego and personality is part of the process of self-realisation. Eventually the integrated consciousness takes over the entire psyche and body and when fully established, all is certainty. This consciousness has access to universal knowledge and all functions on earth, both specific and general, are unmistakably known. The ego's desire to know is finally complete and transcended.

In my experience the taking over of the body by the consciousness was a continuously dramatic experience that lasted for several months. The breathing, heartbeat, movement, the most strenuous exertion was performed in me for 'me' by another yet inseparable me, tirelessly, effortlessly and precisely, even to the point of the body's death. The normal limits of endurance and performance no longer applied. The will performed all the functions.

Everything is based on its function, and function is what is done by the desireless will. The ego's desire to exist is a function of the will. When this is fully realised, all relationship naturally ceases between the ego and desire.

ego *and* experience

THE EGO is an extremely beautiful principle. Its actual function is to protect the organism and organise its knowledge as a moment-to-moment response to the challenge of the environment. It is an avenue of awareness and response.

Ego does not need desire to function. But, like all things, it needs desire to exist. As we have seen, the ego's desire to exist is satisfied by experiencing itself in existence — not just as awareness of the environment but as personality, information and thinking. It supports the personality's interests and whenever the personality is bored or disinterested, the ego continues to affirm its existence (and distract the personality) by thinking. This is where the trouble starts.

While we still have desires the ego cannot deliver a pure response from our being. Every challenge has to pass through the unintegrated personality-ego mechanism. Instead of going straight through as experience of the environment or living, it becomes related to something we want or do not want to happen. We react to the challenge and miss the intense experience of response in our being. Then, instead of seeing what is needed, we project our desires onto the situation and experience the anticipation and tension of desiring — alternating happiness and unhappiness.

The reactivity is what has to go. In other words, all reactions of the personality must disappear, along with our superficiality.

Reaction occurs whenever there is a degree of emotion which is the reciprocal, the tangible going out, of the inner stress of our desiring.

Reaction acts off attitude and occurs wherever there is a degree of emotion. Attitude is a groove formed by previous thinking around a desire. Emotion is an outer expression of the inner stress of the desire; a reciprocal 'motion' outwards.

The more rigid the attitude the more mechanical and faster the reaction. The reactivity soon becomes habitual and the individual is then tiresomely predictable. Reaction is never spontaneous although it might appear to be.

Response is not reaction. Response is spontaneous — a flowing reciprocal movement in which there is no apparent pause, no jarring, no judging. Response unites with every challenge and the result is the expression of harmony.

There are three ways in which man experiences that he exists.

The first is self-assertion, the way of personality and desire for power.

The second is self-affirmation, the way of ego and experience.

The third is self-negation, the way of being as nothing.

It will be seen that these three conditions represent the withdrawal of identity from the coarse extremity of personality, through the assertive experience of the ego, to a self-sufficient point of equanimity and balance — a reducing spiral of noise, imagination and circumstance.

The seeming regression towards 'being nothing' is the withdrawal to a new beginning. The new can only arise from a state of balance, or it will merely be a projection of what was. The 'third man' is a new man, for whom duality has no function.

There is only consciousness and form.

Your real identity is consciousness, not the form you identify with. Consciousness is non-existent so it has no form of its own. You can only know you exist by experiencing the form you take in relation to some other form. That is the form of existence, a state of conscious duality.

The desire to exist is the irresistible impulse of consciousness to experience itself as some form or other; to feel it exists in that form. By 'form' I do not mean just the physical form. That is only one of the many forms you take. The most common form in which you experience yourself is thinking. The subject matter of the thinking is irrelevant. The form is the action of thinking itself.

I have said that consciousness appears as personality in the form of reactions. These forms are as actual as physical ones. They are forms of energy and as such only observable as actions. But as we are taught at school, matter is really energy and the difference is only that physical form is unobservable action, whereas energetic form is observable action.

Because you are consciousness identifying with your form, you identify with your personality. When the personality reacts with emotion, the consciousness steps down into the emotion and enters the world of reactions. In other words, you get emotional. Your ego, however, remains itself — the experience without the emotion. And if you can enter the ego's form — pure uninvolved experience — you can disidentify with the emotion and it can no longer hold its form.

Absence of emotion does not mean absence of sensation. Quite the contrary. In real joy or love there is no emotional reactivity; the sensation of joy is far more beautiful than any emotional feeling. We all know the pleasure of experience without emotion — the simple feeling of being alive or the unobtrusive intensity of being in love.

The ego's experience of life is always pleasant until emotion intervenes. The problem is that man keeps reverting to emotional displays of joy and happiness, and to tears and anger. But even during the most violent emotional outburst the ego-consciousness is looking on, observing the personality's activity as part of its own experience. Because ego is uninvolved during the emotional reaction, man is provided with his only escape route. But it is like a ladder that he must climb up back- wards. Step by step he must resist the enormous pull on him to take the easy way and go back down the rungs of emotion.

Emotion is below the ego's experience. All the machinations, frustrations, triumphs and suffering of the personality merely affirm its own existence. Behind the person the ego is aloof and disinterested, secure in its own uniquely positive feelings, lapping up the experience without the pain.

You might think there can be nothing beyond the ego, because it seems there can be nothing beyond our experience. But this is only true as long as your experience is in relation to something.

Desiring is experienced in relation to what you want; talking in relation to voice; thinking in relation to memory; happiness in relation to acquisition, and so on. These are all forms of experience for the ego but they are partial in relation to the whole continuous experience of living.

Life is not just desiring, talking, thinking, laughing. It is everything — the never-ceasing experience of living. To be 'the third man', beyond the ego-life, you have to experience the experience; that is, be the experience of living without any partiality, emotion or identification. Then you experience the ego by seeing beyond it.

the thinker

WE HAVE SEEN how the ego experiences itself through the wanting and striving of the personality. It also experiences itself as thinking. It does this to fill the gap when you are not attending to something, talking, listening, watching television or reading a book.

When you are thinking you are being communicated to from memory, the storehouse of the past. So in your thoughts you experience impressions created in the past, never the present. Although you are alive, certainly, you are not experiencing being alive.

Ego, as you probably know, means 'I' in Latin. It is a misleading root for the term 'ego' because the ego is 'I being aware of experience'. Put another way, I cannot exist apart from my awareness.

Even more misleading is the often quoted motto: 'I think therefore I am.' This is as illogical as saying 'I see a dog, therefore I am a dog.' It would be better to say: 'I think I think, therefore I think I am' — a conundrum which happens to be the truth.

We think because there is something we want to know. There is also thinking where it seems there is no wanting to know anything. This is the thinking that comes from the ego's desire to know it exists, which is the strongest desire in us. It beams out of us day and night, monitoring the environment for signs of danger. It has to know what is going on to protect us. So there is a continuous reference to memory, evaluating what is seen, heard, smelt and felt. We are unaware of most of this activity — we would go insane if we were — but where it occurs at the conscious level it becomes associative thinking. Thus a letter-box can remind us the gas bill is due and so on. Here, instead of protecting the body, the ego is evaluating the situation in terms of psychological self-interest. This is the ego preserving itself as the desire of the personality. It checks to see that what is 'bad' is resisted and what is 'good' is acquired or embraced; and what is neither good nor bad does not matter. As long as we have the self-interest of desire we will associate with whatever it is through memory and thinking.

Thinking is always the ego's way of experiencing itself in existence. Where a person is too weak to stand alone in a state of not knowing, it props itself up all the time by relating to memory and affirming itself in gossip, discussion, and useless greetings.

The ego is a principle connecting memory with perception; a sort of two-way street of desire, one way pulling in more information, the other punching it out mostly as personality to reaffirm its own knowing or existence.

Thoughts are symbols of past experience stored in memory. It is impossible to have a thought about something you have not experienced. You can imagine, but the image will be an impression built out of what you already know. You cannot imagine my father's kitchen or a new kind of animal without combining bits of information you already have. What we

imagine or build up by thinking will always be a re-arrangement
of the past.

This is what happens: as we perceive the world, sensory
symbols of our experience go into the memory; as we recall
them they come up and associate into the series of thoughts we
call 'thinking'. Thoughts are regurgitations. Thinking is a
slowed down, limited and secondary version of primary
experience.

Anything we perceive that reminds us of an attitude throws
up a related thought out of memory and we begin thinking
about it. The selection mechanism is desire, which as we have
seen is always a tension or stress. Particular thoughts are selected
according to the strength of the tension in the desire. This tension
supplies the energy which links the thoughts into thinking. As
thought begins it generates emotion, a coarse expression of the
tension in the desire; the greater the conflict the greater the hold
of the thought-line and the momentum of the thinking.

We think because we classify things into good and bad, yours
and mine. We select and reject according to our desires and
conditioning which fix the basic attitudes on which we build the
thinker in ourselves. This conditioning begins with my body, my
family, my house; and soon becomes my friends, my enemies,
my country, my beliefs and so on. When we are reminded of
them, we think. And 'good and bad' is what is good and bad for
these things of mine.

Is it possible to live without classifying?

Will our bodies, our families, our countries, be any less safe if
we stop thinking? Are they any less safe at this moment? —
although you are not thinking now, and may never think again.
If someone walks in now and tells you your house is on fire,

you will still take immediate action.

What is this nonsense of thinking all about? We don't use it when we are taking action. We don't use it when we are listening. We certainly don't use it to experience love or the beauty of a sunset.

The fact is that we think when we are unconscious of being alive, when we have lost contact with reality. Thinking is us dreaming while we imagine we are awake. And most of our talking is also dreaming — expressed in words instead of thoughts.

The question is: How do we know when our thinking and talking is dreaming? And the answer is, when we are avoiding the fact.

(Follow this closely, because at this moment you are experiencing the truth of what is being said. You are looking for the fact. So you are neither thinking nor talking.)

Avoiding the fact is escapism. Thinking and most of our talking is an attempt to escape from the fact of life. This is a difficult and painful fact to face because it means the end of us as self-assertive, self-affirming entities. By thinking, talking and discussing we try to run away from the fact.

A fact can only be faced by living it.
You do not have to think or talk.
Just live it. Now.
Unless you grasp this fact instantly you are wasting your time.

We use the word thinking to describe a mental process that has two distinct functions. One is thinking as a form of dreaming. The other we use when we make plans or look to see what the situation is. The difference between planning and thinking is that when we plan we use only facts and always with the intention at that moment of translating them into action.

Action is the reality. We all know it is a world of facts which will mercilessly crush anyone who acts on airy-fairy notions and impressions. Realising this, whenever we have anything important to do, we look at the situation and take action. And when we want to escape into waking sleep (which includes worry) we think, or exchange dreams in talking.

I am not saying it is wrong to think or have discussions. There is no right or wrong in this — only finding the fact. 'Right and wrong', like 'good and bad' are judgments based on conditioned attitudes. If you have no attitude to what you are doing, when you look at a situation you see only the fact.

The optimum of man's experience is beyond thinking and talking as a need.

When someone begins to see this, will he or she settle for anything less than the total, enduring experience?

Is this not the movement of life — always towards the greater experience?

And what of those who do not see this truth, or do not believe it, are they wrong?

You might have long periods of stillness and then suddenly find yourself thinking again. Why?

As we have already seen, thinking is a habit deeply ingrained in us by desire. When desire goes it leaves behind a furrow or groove along which we continue to think, sometimes much to the annoyance of someone who has experienced stillness. This 'groove-thinking' is sporadic and can be fairly quickly starved out. Although it doesn't have the virulence of desire (rather the strength of a persistent idea) it is still pretty painful to obliterate the groove.

If you experience the fact that thinking is a form of sleep you will begin to wake up. You will think less and less. But if you have only followed this self-discovery intellectually, or even if you agree with me, you will go on thinking just as much as ever.

the talker

"I WOULD LIKE to question you about some of the things you've said and discuss a few of the points with you, if you don't mind."

Go ahead. If you have a question, it means you have not yet seen the fact, or the truth behind it. But remember that you have to experience the fact or truth of what I'm saying, not just the words.

It is easy to get imprisoned in words. We have to introduce reality into what we are saying, to give it substance, to make sure it is a fact.

"First of all, your definition of 'thinking' seems rather limited. I would have thought there's more to it than just day-dreaming and planning. And secondly, you seem to want to get rid of the beauty of imagination . . ."

Is day-dreaming beautiful? Is it beautiful to imagine yourself in a pleasant situation that's not happening and probably never will?

If that's your idea of beauty, there is nothing wrong with it. But if you look closer you will see it is self-delusion; and the only beauty of it is escapism. When the same sort of thinking is about an unpleasant situation we call it worry.

"All the same, thinking seems much more real than dreaming . . ."

Reality is now, so we have to look at 'thinking' from the continuously moving point of this moment, and that's not easy.

This is vitally important. Unless you continue to relate thinking to this moment, to your own experience of 'now' as action, you will not understand it; you will only think you do. Then you will actually exist as thinking; and thinking, like anger, can never understand itself.

There is no 'thinking' and 'you'. When you think, you are the thinking.

You have to grasp this fact: When you are engaged in thinking, you are the thinker; when you are angry, you are anger; when you are desiring, you are desire; and so on. When you are none of these things, when you are not acting from anything that can be named, you are as nothing. And, in that moment, you experience reality.

If you grasp this, you will see that thinking always comes after the moment of perception.

But do not dwell on what I've said or you will start to think and miss what's coming. If you have a need to reflect on it later, you will do so without effort. But in order to listen now, while it is new, you have to keep moving, never pausing, so that you experience the fact of what is being said and not just the words, which is what happens in discussions.

"I cannot believe that discussion is wrong."

By making that statement you're trying to start a discussion, because you're telling me what you believe. If someone else were here and told you what he believes about it, you would both be able to get the satisfaction of asserting yourselves in a discussion. And you would soon be talking about things you know nothing about.

Look, you are endeavouring to know yourself, which leads towards the experience of being nothing — absence of belief, absence of discussion, absence of desire and absence of trying.

"But aren't you discussing these things?"

I am talking. But if you are listening properly, I am destroying your need to assert yourself, not satisfying it.

"Okay. I am trying to follow you. But it's difficult, especially as you say I should not be trying!"

'Not trying' is different from 'absence of trying'. To either try or not try requires a positive and self-assertive attitude. To be absence of trying is to be as nothing.

"Well, why would I want to be nothing?"

To 'want to be nothing' is pointless; because whatever wants (or doesn't want) can never be nothing.

"But presumably I have to want to stop wanting?"

You cannot want to stop wanting, or even aim to cease desiring. That would be a working of desire. But you can observe desire in yourself in all the moments of desiring. And then you can begin to see how it works.

"But you must agree that to do anything there has to be the desire to do it. So if I decide to sit down and meditate I have to have the desire to meditate, for example."

Do you?

While you desire to meditate you are not meditating. How can you do anything and desire to do it at the same time?

"It's impossible; that's right. There has to be a desire first. For example, I have to desire to go to work before I can go to work tomorrow."

Then let's get rid of you as desire and see if you still go to work tomorrow.

"Well, yes. I'll just eat my breakfast and go. But you're not answering me. I am saying that in order to ask you any of these questions I had to desire to ask them."

No, you didn't. You just asked the questions.

"But I 'thought' beforehand."

Only if you were trying to be clever. Then you desired to assert yourself and you had to think. If you were being intelligent and sincere you simply observed in yourself a lack of comprehension and spoke from there.

Observation, or awareness, always contains its own effortless movement of response. That's how you get out of the way of a moving car, or stop a closing door from slamming, without having to think about it first.

When we are aware of a lack of comprehension in ourselves, at the same time we observe what is needed to dispel it. So we ask a question, or keep listening. Or we continue to observe what we understand in relation to what we don't; which is the reflection that continually supplies our solutions. There is no desire involved, so there is no thinking.

"I still do not understand. Say I decide to meditate. I have to stop doing what I'm doing and go and sit down. I must desire to stop what I am already doing."

The only thing you will stop doing is thinking. Meditation is 'not thinking'.

"So does meditation stop desire?"

Where there is no thought, there is no desire. So in meditation there is absence of desire.

You cannot think while you are aware and observing yourself. So meditation is observation. If you are doing the ironing and not thinking, you are participating with your body in moment-to-moment action. Your body is acting and you are observing; the result is the experience called awareness. This is meditation, whatever you are doing.

Meditation is a desireless state of mind, awareness in action without thought. But the state cannot be imagined, because if I try to imagine something I act out of desire. And desire cannot know the desireless.

If you are listening intelligently there is a possibility that you will suddenly recognise a description of yourself in action; and in that moment, if it is a living experience and not a conclusion, you will understand. But you have to follow what is being said as your own experience of being desire. If you try to follow me with your mind, with what you have read or what you believe, or from any point of accumulated knowledge, you will not understand. You will merely add to your attitudes and be further away from the truth.

"Are you saying that attitudes have no value at all?"

Surely the first question is: Why do we have attitudes? Why do we need these psychological possessions — ideas, opinions, attitudes? Why do we find it necessary to carry around all these secretions of stale thought?

Why can't we meet every challenge as ourselves, as we are? Do we feel we have to recall what we like and don't like? Or can we discover life fresh and new at every moment, not in thought, but in the sheer sensation of being alive?

Attitudes and opinions are part of self-assertion, which is a device to give us a false sense of continuity. To understand this you must observe yourself while you are expressing your attitudes and opinions.

Man lives in two distinct worlds, see-sawing all the time between one and the other. One is the world of moment-to-moment awareness and response, when man experiences the pure experience of living. In this he has no psychological continuity and needs none. He exists as the experience. As there is no thought and no trying, there is no experience of time. The other is a world of assertion and self-affirmation, and satisfaction which is always a sign of self-affirmation. Feelings of satisfaction or dissatisfaction follow reference to a past event, thinking, and therefore are in time and subject to change. So these are the two worlds: the timeless experience of living and the timed experience of satisfaction.

When do you express your attitudes and opinions? When do you act out your memories? When you are engaged in useless conversations. By 'useless' I mean any conversation from which you get satisfaction.

"So, if I am serious about working on myself, would it be a good idea to give up talking?"

Why would you ask that question? Why would anyone ask if they should give up talking? The question arises only because you do not understand talking. If you understood, the question would be unnecessary so useless talking would not occur. And in that sense some talking would have been given up.

You do not ask why you breathe: you understand the experience of breathing. If you understood everything would you ever have the need to speak? You might — we cannot say that you would not — but would you ever have the need to speak as a desire to find the fact? Of course not. If you understand you know the fact. Where there is knowledge there are no questions. So to the degree that you understand talking you will cease talking as the need to talk.

"But it's my understanding that I have to try to change things about myself and I have to make a positive decision to give something up."

You have to understand the self-created problem of deciding to give things up, of trying to change yourself. By trying, you substitute one conflict for another.

How can you try to not get angry?

What you mean, if you say that, is that you will try not to express your anger. But at the moment of trying you are already anger. So your trying is merely the same anger trying to control itself; a hopeless proposition that leaves a scalding conflict within you.

Like talking and thinking, anger has to be understood and then there is no need of it, for you.

"So the clue to all this is in the word 'need'?"

Need is a word that is rarely understood.

While you have a psychological need of anything you are not self-sufficient.

The need to talk is our greatest crutch.

"Does that mean that there comes a time in the spiritual life when talking ceases?"

Can you cease talking in the future? Is there an element of time in the ceasing of talking?

Or did you cease talking after you last spoke? And are you now, at this moment, absence of talking, which is timeless?

Can you see the enormous significance of this?

Can you see that whenever you introduce the future tense into talking you project yourself into time? In time there is no ceasing of questions, talking, fear or anything else.

Is it possible for you to live without talking about the future?

I cannot answer that for you and I cannot answer it for myself. For if I speak I will be in time. But if I live my answer, my understanding of what is being said, there is no speaking about the future; I am that absence and so I am timeless.

It must be clear from this that talking and thinking about what we intend to do, as distinct from doing it, projects us into time, into the waking sleep of living. Talking and thinking create time. And action (as absence of talking and thinking) is timelessness or the continuous present — now.

Looking and listening properly is this timelessness in action. You act without an object. You attend on the subject and the facts just appear in your mind.

When you have an object, such as wanting to be 'spiritual' or honest or good or kind, you act on your impression of what it means to you and not on the fact; for example what it is to be honest — and not the fact of being honest. So all you achieve is your own idea of honesty, a terrifying piece of self-delusion.

"Isn't there always an object for every action?"

While there is the idea of 'a subject' there will always be the idea of 'an object'. But if I am the subject — 'I'— the idea of 'an object' disappears and only the fact remains.

The problem for the mind is that 'I' am not a fact. The body is a fact; memory is a fact; sensation is a fact; action is a fact. But 'I' am not a fact that can be substantiated objectively — except as a conflict. In the same way as honesty is an idea produced by the opportunity to be dishonest, 'I' am an idea of myself and I exist only in relation to what I am not. I have no continuity, for example, except in relation to memory. Have I?

However, do you build a bridge where there is no need of one? Do you do anything where there is no need? When you act intelligently don't you first see the need for the action? Is not the need the fact?

When you see the fact that a bridge or crossing is needed, you act to build one. Where is the idea in this? There is only the seeing of the fact and the necessary action. And then there is the chance of something new.

You have ideas when you cannot see the fact or are not looking for it. Then you discuss them and get further and further away from the fact or the need of action.

"Are you going to take ideas away from me now? Ideas are as important or more important to me than facts. Surely we need our ideas . . ."

Isn't need always the need for action?

Action is facts in motion.

Is there anything more infuriating than a person who won't stick to the facts when you're preparing to take action?

The injured man, the traffic jam, the broken window, the unwritten book, the ripe crop, next week's rent, the queue outside the cinema — aren't these all a need indicating action?

What ideas or discussions do you need to help the injured man? He doesn't need your ideas or what you believe. He needs the best you can do for him, whatever that is. And his need will drag it out of you in the form of spontaneous action.

"So spontaneous action is a pure response to need, without any idea in it."

Yes, action without idea is action without an object; without the presence of an 'I' as a separate idea of myself. Where there is pure action, there is just the pure perception of the situation exactly as it is.

To see everything exactly as it is would be to give up every idea, every classification of experience in the mind. Everything is constantly different, changing far faster than human perception can know. We slow down our awareness to classify our experience and put it into words. Then we see the words and ideas in place of everything just as it is. But in pure perception there is not 'a tree' any more than there is 'a man' — or an 'I' to perceive it.

To see everything as clearly as this would mean the disappearance of our dependence on others as psychological props; and the need to talk and communicate our ideas in words would diminish. As the fact of our self-sufficiency became known, the dreaming world of ideas, words and discussions would gradually give way to a dynamic world of action and perception.

The pinnacle of pure action is not physical. The swiftest, most beautiful action in the world is that of consciousness being love and knowledge. That is the consciousness that's dawning in you.

response and reaction

MAN REACTS or responds to the world according to how deeply an idea or impulse penetrates him.

I am going to give you a model of man in which there are seven levels of reaction or response, as follows:

1. Physical reaction
2. Thought
3. Attitude
4. Feeling
5. Knowledge
6. Sensation
7. Being

There is a natural sequence from the first to the seventh so an impulse from the world travels from the physical towards the level of being until it stops in any one of the levels. And as this is a two-way street the response or reaction travels back to the world through the levels in sequence. Where it stops depends on the responsiveness of the individual.

The level of thoughts is also that of words and images and is the place of aimless thought and talking.

The level of attitude is a little deeper. Here man reacts from his attitudes and opinions and their mass lends weight and firmness to his words and thoughts in the level above. Here are man's political and religious beliefs.

Arguments begin here as man reacts from his 'centres'. A centre is any idea, any bit of the past that has not been allowed to die — an attitude to anything, a concept of what it is to be good or courteous, an ideal of decency, morality, peace or any such tiresome word.

Centres are like bricks in man's perception, accumulations of rigidity formed in his experience, out of which he builds what he calls his mind, but which is actually his superficial self.

'Mind' is not the substantive entity man often thinks it is. It is a function identical with the multiplication sign in mathematics. The function is the judging or classifying of things by comparing them with the 'self-centres'. And out of this multiplication sum comes the infinite product of talking or thinking without purpose or design.

The man-machine, like every machine, is itself a centre with a capacity for only limited response. No matter how big or complex you make a machine, or how much information you pour into a computer, it remains a centre of limited response.

Next is the level of desire and emotion where man keeps what he calls his 'feelings'. Man acts from his feelings when there is desire in him, or opposition to the self-centres in the level above. He reacts from here as desire when he either sees or comprehends that there is something he wants. And he reacts from here when he can't have it. This is the ground of violent argument and anger.

At Level Five is knowledge. A response to the world from knowledge eliminates all the feelings, beliefs, attitudes and thinking in the levels above. It therefore eliminates man as a reactionary principle and as 'mind'. This is the beginning of responsive man.

Acting from here man responds to the world without reaction. Travelling back out to the world through the other levels his response transforms desire and emotion with a much finer energy, which is turn dissolves the attitudes, rigidity and argument. It eliminates the need of words and thoughts, finally appearing in the body as a smile, gesture or an act of understanding.

As knowledge passes through desire and emotion it appears as love, although where there is wanting in the love, it remains a personal and selfish love.

At its finest, knowledge acts with conscious perception. A person acting with such perception obviously acts without a centre; because it is far below the level of centres. Conscious perception has no home of bricks, no fixtures from which to judge and multiply a spurious future, no limiting apertures of expectation. As it passes through man's centres it eliminates them, crosses out the errors in the mind's multiplication system and allows the equation to work itself out.

Conscious perception is understanding and memory, plus action. Passing through the level of words and thoughts, it appears as spontaneous response and freedom of expression.

Level Six is sensation, or feeling purified of any identity as emotion or desire. This is the place of impersonal love, beauty and joy — feeling without an object. As love or joy passes from here through the levels below, it transforms each of them in turn. At the peak of love's expression, the silent action of presence alone communicates directly and unsuspected to another person who is able to respond to it in the level below; who will know it as impersonal love or truth.

Level Seven is being; consciousness acting as pure perception, entirely responsive but with no need to exist as anything more than an expression of God's will.

Man's highest perception is unlimited in response, and that is everlasting life or immortality.

For Superficial Man the impulses of the world reach only as far as his feelings. And his life is a reaction to the world.

Responsible Man is responsive man. And when he always acts from conscious perception he is truly responsible for his life.

A strange thing happens when man becomes a responsible being. He no longer needs the world to pull responses out of him.

Whereas Superficial Man reacts into the world as an effect, Responsible Man acts into the world as a cause. His knowledge actually destroys the effects that Superficial Man creates with his reactions. His understanding dissolves the reactions of fear, hate, anger, envy, argument and lust for power — as you have seen for yourself when you are understanding. Whereas Superficial Man is creator of these reactions, Responsible Man is destroyer of them. One complicates, the other simplifies.

When you destroy through reaction you leave behind hostility, hate, opposition, war — and more reaction. When you destroy through understanding, for a little while you leave behind peace or love or joy.

Joy is not a reaction. It is a response. It is a part of the action which caused it and needs no display. Joy is sensation without an object; in other words, it is not a feeling attached to any notion of good or bad, or any centre.

Using the model of man's levels of reaction and response, we can see how Superficial Man reacts to the possibility of joy. The first reaction is in the body; a noise of some sort, excitement, laughter, handshakes. Then come words: 'Isn't it wonderful!' — the sudden windfall or the birth of a baby — 'We'll be so happy now!' Then attitude: 'But we'll have to be sensible with the money'; or 'We must raise him as a Catholic.' Then emotion: the imagined feeling of power or pride; or, when opposition to desire is encountered or imagined, a hardening insistence or vengeance — 'I'll show him.'

In Responsible Man joy creates no reaction but a response of love which he feels within himself and emanates in silence. In the body his joy may appear as a smile, though seldom more than a smile for those around him who do not yet know the bliss of love as pure sensation beyond display.

Joy cannot be celebrated. To celebrate joy by dancing is to enjoy dancing; by drinking to enjoy drinking; by talking to enjoy talking. Let the dancers dance, the feasters feast and the talkers talk — for they are truly a joy in themselves. But the joy of a marriage, the birth of a child, the love of another is in the silence of your own being, where your need of the world ends — and the world's need of you begins.

While you want anything in the world you are reacting.

What is the implication of this for you, in your life? It does not mean that you should give up working, eating, buying a car or enjoying yourself. It means you do those things without the desire to do them; and without the desire not to do them. To not desire something is as positive a reaction as to desire it.

If nothing is desired and nothing is not desired there is a state of equilibrium. The result is the act of going to work, eating, enjoyment, buying food or cars, and all the rest of living — without having the terrible fight of reaction when things change, are threatened or come to an end. Reaction occurs when there is a change and as life consists of change the opportunity for reaction occurs every second.

Reaction is the desire to cling to the past or resist the new. It is most noticeable when the change means that something is taken from you which you once desired or now want to hold on to.

You react and suffer according to the strength of your desire. And when you gain something, if you react in joy you can be sure that when change comes again, as it must, you will react in unhappiness. Each reaction in your life is an over-correction of your course, making a future correction inevitable.

Reaction is a striving for certainty. As certainty does not exist in the world, reaction becomes a striving to produce certainty within its own activity. This requires a continual narrowing and reduction of flexibility which appears as frowning watchfulness, exclusion, suppression and rejection. Anything new is soon converted back into the familiar.

This fundamental movement is common to both individuals and society as a whole. The tendency is always to preserve what exists and return to some form of conservatism. Even rebellions are led by reactionaries, and the same law applies. Young rebels become householders. Revolutionaries overturn the Old Order and quickly adopt their own hardline.

In both individual and society, every reaction is initially (and moment to moment) an attempt to hold on to something, whether it be an object, idea or attitude. Once the threat or challenge is over, the person or society tries to respond from the new sense of assurance. But pure response is impossible. A gesture from a position of security is still a reaction of security, an extension and modification of itself. A true response on the other hand is a spontaneous action, with no consideration of anything, not even its own comfort or survival (unless the success depends on those considerations).

This tendency towards self-preservation produces familiar social phenomena: the sprawling in-breeding of complication; a stifling proliferation of rules, laws, attitudes and opinions; the ever-tightening mesh of self-spawned rigidity surrounding a sickly-soft centre; a 'progress' that is nothing more than self-poisoning; a drying up, a shrinking towards ultimate seizure and immobility.

It is obvious that the world would eventually seize up if it ran on man's reactivity alone. The need for security would eventually destroy man and his society. But of course they are not allowed to rest secure. There is another far greater energy at work, an irresistible action. Instead of arising out of reaction in man, or an impulse from the world bouncing back into the world, this energy acts directly into the world from the deepest level of being, where man has his origins. To reactive Superficial Man it is a disruptive force bent on disunity and destruction. But understood with knowledge, or viewed from the conscious perception, it is the other half of the story, essential to life's purpose. It is opposed to the world; to conservation and preservation. It's what keeps putting the space back in between the proliferating habitual forms of life, making room for movement and tolerance in the world. It is insecurity, uncertainty and the blessed wind of change. Death. Or, by another name, love.

making space

SPONTANEOUS RESPONSE and habitual reaction are the two opposing forces that operate simultaneously in man and often cause him deep-seated conflict. In respect to a single action, they can run absolutely counter to each other. In those moments man finds himself doing what he knows to be certain folly, even disaster; but he can't stop himself.

The honest man finds himself being dishonest. The thief owns up against his will. The loving mother leaves home. The spotless priest commits an act of indecency. Healthy people find themselves dying and can't believe it; (nothing surprises superficial man more than the prospect of his own death). On and on it goes: the unexpected, the contrary, the new and the News; the most astonishing item of News being that the newspaper readers and TV viewers are actually surprised by it all, day after day, year in and year out.

All these situations mean the death of some previous condition. The new always follows the death of something. But to see what death is in its totality you have to adjust your vision. We cannot confine death by saying it is simply the absence of organic life. Absence of life is impossible.

What we call 'life' in living things is actually reaction. What we call 'death' is change, the end of a particular series of reactions, the coming of a new series. Each moment must die to make way for the next. The next step can only occur when a previous position is destroyed or dies.

When the heart stops beating and the blood ceases to circulate, the body ceases to react in the way we call life. But in that limited sense what a misnomer the word 'life' is! As a corpse, the entire body now responds to the spontaneous and irresistible action of decay, that essential part of life that establishes new conditions. From the disintegrating corpse death provides the new as organic matter. For those attached to the dead body, it brings the psychologically new.

Death is the space before and after life. There is more space than matter, more death than life, more silence than noise.

Death is the condition of life. Every reaction is a consequence of the death of some thing or state. Life is reaction. Death is the response.

This response or flow of death through man and all things into the world is like a deep river. The direction and massive power of the flow is unchangeable but on the surface the winds and ripples of reaction seem to give the surface an appearance of independent movement.

If consciousness identifies itself with the surface it imagines the conflicting interaction of the winds, eddies and ripples to be 'life'; the depths below are relatively static and void of interest.

Until man becomes this deep, silent, irresistible response, this timeless governor of change and life, he must dance and limp and fight and die on the surface of his being.

When man finds himself going against what he really wants to do, his deeper self is making him break an attitude or habit that he has temporarily identified with.

Take the example of a man who lives by stealing from others. He is identified with a centre of reaction in himself that gives rise to the attitude and mentality of a thief. Every challenge from his environment that relates to his need of material things must go first through this centre. Soon the pattern becomes habit. But eventually the death-force acts through the thief and he confesses or gets caught; or in some other way life destroys or frustrates the 'thief' in him. Not because stealing is wrong. There is no right or wrong at this level. But because all attitudes or centres are false. They corrupt and distort the pure perception of which man is capable and they retard the achievement of that exalted consciousness to which the whole of life is striving.

The thief, as much as any one of us, is pure perception first and thief second. The thief must be destroyed as a centre of reaction to the environment. In the same way as the honest man, the good parent, the pious priest, the fit and healthy man, the famous doctor, the faithful wife, the successful, the unsuccessful, the poor, the rich, must all be destroyed once these ideas become 'positions' or fixed centres of reaction in any person, state or thing. Nothing lasts; everything is being pulled down, eroded, changed. Especially is this so in man, whose suffering and misery is nothing more than the destruction of some attitude or centre which is trying to use him and 'be him' — whereas man is really nothing but the space and perception that acts through all things, acting through particular brains and bodies.

A man might be a thief, a doctor, a poet, a father, a pianist. He is each of these things at the moment of being it. But if he tries to be one while performing as another he will cease acting and begin reacting. That is, the moment-to-moment action of what he is doing will react off another aspect of himself which will quickly result in inefficiency and produce a centre of stress, irritation or anger. This is what is happening whenever we feel emotion.

Take the example of a doctor who is frustrated or worried, which means he has gone beyond the pure act of being a doctor and is reacting off a false centre. It is this centre that the death-force is intent on destroying; not the spontaneous, untroubled activity of the man going about his profession but any centre of reaction, emotion and attitude in him.

The man is the vehicle for the function. 'Doctor' exists as a function, moment to moment. When the man is not the doctor, he is another function such as father, liar, lover, host, husband, householder, bore.

A person can only exist as any function from moment to moment. A man who declares that come what may he will adhere to the Hippocratic Oath of Physicians, and thinks he really means it, is in danger of establishing a centre in himself that death must later smash. He will react off it and know conflict, or actually be driven to break his oath. But it cannot exist for him as a centre or attitude if he takes the oath knowing that he may or may not break it according to the moment. Then he is free.

Sworn oaths do not govern man's behaviour. But fear as a centre can — the fear of punishment by the law, ostracism or loss of status. In most people these things are part of their understanding of the way of things and they no longer need to refer to a code of behaviour to dictate their moment-to-moment action. But if the deeper self makes them transgress there will probably be a centre in them sensitive to what they think others may think or say; they will react from there and suffer shame, remorse or regret. They will react to the reaction of other people's reactions. The pain of it comes to break up any centre in man that he tries to preserve as a limitation of his illimitable being.

Attitudes and centres are ignorance; clots of self in the pure stream of perception and spontaneous action. They are dissolved by first seeing that they are there; and second, by examining their basis as they assert themselves in some form of reaction. When you discover the original false assumption on which each attitude is grounded you automatically discard the whole accumulation.

Man cannot usually do this, because he actually believes he is his centres or positions. So he says: 'I'm a Roman Catholic' or 'I'm a Socialist' and 'I believe in . . .' When man is so identified with his centres that he cannot dissolve them for himself, the death-force must do it for him. The result is the tension of argument, frustration, disappointment, disenchantment, doubt, boredom, unpleasantness — all signs of the slow attrition of some centre or position. For life knows that eventually enough pain will make even the most stupid person look for the cause in himself.

Man's reactivity produces all that is complicated, ugly and artificial. All that is worthwhile and beautiful is produced by the spontaneous, responsive life-force that drives into the world through man. The death-force is simply life's response when man tries to cling to anything as a position or centre in himself.

Man is not doctor or thief any more than he is the father or the liar. He is all the things that he can do and be. But to be able to respond freely, competently and beautifully to whatever the moment demands he must be himself; that is, remain as nothing but the still, perceptive space between every action.

Man is the meeting point of a thousand reactions, a mirror for the face of the world. But as pure response without a centre he is all the things that he is — a spontaneous whole, combining life and death in a world behind reaction. When he performs any action with sincerity he has no centre; he is the experience and the uninterrupted unemotional response of his perception.

FIVE

TO BE THE MASTER OF YOURSELF MEANS HAVING the continuous certainty that every moment of your life, even the moment of death, is your own will.

To be the master of your mind means having a three hundred and sixty degree awareness without a centre. This remarkable expansion of perception brings an effortless, moment-to-moment unfoldment of self-knowledge. When it emerges from the consciousness in the form of facts about man and his existence, this knowledge is a tapping of the universal memory, past, present and so-called future, which is all in you — now.

The highest teaching occurs in the silence, in the presence of a person of this exalted consciousness. His or her words, spoken or written, no matter how perceptive, are secondary to the living of them.

To be sure that what you discover in these pages is yours and not just something someone else has written, you have to be very still. Remember to read without thinking you know anything. Look at what is being said in your own experience as you read. If you refer to memory, even for a moment, you will miss the fact and end up with words and a debatable theory — not the truth. What I say is true only in terms of self-knowledge; in words and writing it is delusion.

absence of experience

IF THE WORLD were removed, and nothing was substituted for it, it would obviously be the end of man's existence. He would still have a memory full of information but nothing actual to relate it to.

The world is a device to pull man's knowledge out of him. Without a world there would be no movement in man's mind between his perception and the data in his memory. For normal man this would seem a complete absence of experience, an appalling loneliness. For some it could mean suicide, madness or schizophrenia.

Temporary absence of experience, however, is a common condition. I was not just using words when I said 'If the world were removed', because that is exactly what happens. The world is removed, though not completely and permanently.

Our world consists of our experience of it. The objects in it are not our world. It is our experience of the objects that makes them real. So to remove the world from a man all you have to do is remove his experience of it. You might say that an obvious way of doing this would be to kill him. That of course removes the man, but not the world, which in death continues to exist although the ability to experience it vanishes.

Absence of experience is familiar to everyone in their own

lives to some degree. It occurs very frequently when you try to do something because it is 'good' for you or expected of you although you are not really interested in doing it. The action communicates nothing to you but the void which you know as boredom.

Or, if you have fallen out of love with someone and you try to continue the relationship instead of ending it, the former lover's presence or touch can leave you cold; you are already on the alert for someone new to come along and give you the chance to re-experience love.

The incidence of 'absence of experience' in fact covers the whole range of man's activities and is the basis of his superficial development, his maturing personality. But total absence of experience over a period of months or years is very rare.

Complete absence of experience can occur in people who go on to kill themselves.

Some suicides destroy themselves as a desperate unconscious attempt to regain experience; or as an imagined means of overcoming the terrible agony of its absence.

And some people kill themselves psychologically by allowing the absence of experience to destroy their dependence on the stimuli of the world. These mystics (as I will call them here) are impelled to rise above existence as a reaction to the world and so participate in the realisation of consciousness.

In a case of schizophrenia the ego is in some way deprived of the experience of relationships; normal or necessary experience is absent to some degree. To allow it to experience itself, the ego splits superficially into two or more separate entities and creates a substitute for the normal experience of the world.

As the ego divides its surface identity and forms new

personalities, experience of the world returns and it is as though a new person is born. This is such an intense and abnormal experience that the response to the world and behaviour is erratic and unpredictable; there is the danger of anti-social reaction. But at the same time perception is elevated. The person may experience different aspects of reality and the psychic world, making statements and performing actions that to the normal perception range from the eccentric to the insane.

The condition of schizophrenia can loosely be termed an overdose of perception. Visions, inner voices, clairvoyance, psychic perception of colours, energies and odours; the dissolution of the body or other objects; knowledge of death and the significance of worldly experience — all this may occur in the exalted state of consciousness. Many experiences are beyond reason and utterance.

All mystics in the process of realisation must eventually pass through the state of no experience, remaining consciously aware of what is happening. That is the difference between the mystic and the mental patient.

Mystics may have abnormal perceptions, higher knowledge and transcendent experiences but their normal faculties remain intact. They are able to adapt their behaviour to acceptable standards within the normal frame of reference while seeing things as they really are. In extreme cases, this requires a delicate balance. But the living of that balance may produce a teacher of truth.

The absence of relationship which causes schizophrenia is an uncontainable loneliness and a person who is not sufficiently prepared to undergo it may go insane — be unable to return to normality at will. But mystics who go through the schizophrenic experience are able to maintain their equilibrium because their progress along the way (described in this book) is a preparation for it. From the very first moment of turning within, they begin to sever relationships (as a need) with things, states or persons outside themselves.

Practising meditation and self-observation is further preparation. Through self-observation and the practice of non-reaction over the years the mystic disidentifies with the surface personality, gradually withdraws and becomes one with the pure ego. From this place within himself he watches the day-to-day ups and downs of the personality. He becomes increasingly aloof to its wavering moods, and its transitory pleasures and pains.

In the final stages, when life really applies the pressure, the mystic feels pain as the personality is mercilessly hammered, for his disidentification with it is not yet complete. But because of his preparation he will always have the certain knowledge that he is also something else — the stable ego. He will retain the conviction that allows him to hold on to sanity through any suffering.

This is the point of realisation where some mystics hold on to God; or as they pass through it, become 'God' — the pure ego, which all along has been supporting the consciousness in the body.

When disidentification from the surface personality is complete the ego is seen as God. But this is still not the state of complete realisation. When the individual knows himself as being beyond any reaction to the world, all-immersed but non-involved, as the principle of love itself, God disappears as anything to be or become.

existing as nothing

TO BE BEYOND thinking and talking as a need, to be beyond desiring, to cease to have a need of psychological continuity, is to exist as nothing.

If you have ever woken up suddenly and startled in the middle of the night, you will have an idea of what this means. There is often a brief moment of terrifying uncertainty about where you are and what you are. In that moment you experience existence without memory and without sense perception; you are absence of body, world and psychological continuity. If only you had enough time you would perceive this absence of relationship as 'being nothing' and 'being nowhere'.

The situation just described only approximates to the state of being in which 'I exist as nothing'. The waking sleeper still relates to something outside himself; he wants to know where he is. The pure state of being is an unimaginable self-sufficiency dependent on no relationship outside itself. Even the relationship to knowledge disappears and what is left is just what is.

For anyone to be plunged suddenly into the state of nothing would be a diabolical, disintegrating experience. We have only to experience the loss of a relatively small relationship, like a person we love, to understand what it would mean to suddenly lose our relationship to everything — friends, money, job, family, honour, possessions and living itself; but that is what it means to exist as nothing. So it is done gradually by the great movement of life. And those who still have beliefs and need their opinions and discussions are spared from seeing the truth too quickly; they go the gradual way of gradual understanding and graduated experience.

You will be alone when you discover the secret of death. And you will be alone when you discover the secret of life.

When desire and relationships are sufficiently smashed, the individual realises immortality. This is a psychological transition in that the fear of death, the fearing entity in the person, goes forever.

The experience can be preceded by the sense that death is near. This is so convincing that a man may give instructions about what is to be done with his personal belongings when it happens. He apprehends the pending death as physical, although the body is not involved in this realisation.

The experience is quite different from the mystical experience of oneness with nature, which brings a conviction about the fact of immortality. The realisation is a participation in the fact, not just the seeing of it, and brings a knowledge that remains forever, because the desire-pattern is too weak to ever interfere again. In the mystical experience the desire-pattern is only temporarily suspended, so the conviction is retained mainly as an intellectual formulation, and fear remains.

Because there is no death as we imagine it, the person in the realisation does not comprehend immediately that he has died or passed through death. All he comprehends is that there is no death; only everlasting life. But then, if he looks back he realises he is 'dead' — the point of death being only the conflict between what he knew before and what he knows now.

The death-state is absence of experience, an interval of most distressing confusion. In my experience it lasted for about six weeks. On the one hand I had the unshakable knowledge of the fact of individual immortality; on the other hand, in the world, terrible indecision, lack of direction and unbelievable desirelessness. The simplest decision, even which side of the bed to get out of, could become an agony of suspense and uncertainty. Then came the rebirth, the indescribable experience of being new. And indecision gave way to an integrated knowledge of certainty and delight, of individual function and unity of life's purpose.

Each phase of realisation appears complete in itself, but there is no conclusion to the realisation of consciousness. The next phase for me came three years later with the transcendental realisation.

In this state there is a distinct possibility of physical death. At one point my perception watched the heartbeats and breathing cease and observed the body continuing to survive independent of both functions.

The watching was done not by a separate entity looking down on the body from a spatial position in external space, as happens in out-of-the-body experiences. The perception can only be described as 'integral awareness'. Its environment is the real body/being. To this perception physical death is neither material nor immaterial.

I mention the stopping of the heart and breathing, a very minor part of this vast realisation, to illustrate the personal drama involved. The experiences in this realisation are so abnormal, varied and continuous that to write of them out of the context of my life would be to test the credulity of the most sympathetic imagination.

I lost 16 lbs weight in five days and ate nothing substantial for six weeks. For six months the body was kept at about 20 lbs below average weight despite a large intake of starch-rich foods, normally a dietary disaster for me. Several people enquired if I was dying. The weight loss and emaciation were not caused by lack of food, but by the release of a new energy which causes metamorphosis in the physical and desire bodies. During the critical period the energy itself substituted for food and maintained a remarkable reservoir of strength for the body, despite its starved and sick appearance. Sleep as a physical need almost disappeared and became a new dimension of perception beyond the dream-world. In the awake state the perception was taken beyond reason, beyond continuity, where nothing exists as itself.

The realisation is called 'transcendental' because the perception looks into the creation as though from outside and suddenly knows itself in relation to the complementary but lesser function of love, the Creator.

possibilities alone

MAN MUST LEARN to live in possibilities alone.

While he has the attitude that even his next footstep is certain he will operate from a centre. When he exists in a state of knowing nothing all attitudes are automatically dissolved.

This sounds like amnesia; and in a way it is, except that amnesia is involuntary loss of memory whereas what I am talking about is a permanent action of will that eliminates all unwanted reference to memory.

When there is no reference to memory there is no knowing.

Let us look at this a little closer. To know you know something there first has to be a conflict in you, a wanting to know. All you know is kept in your memory. If you cut off from memory you cannot know what you know. All you perceive is what is happening now. You then perform as a pure response to the situation. You do not need to use your memory except for checking facts when you are planning or looking at a situation. That takes only a small part of your day. The rest of the time could be spent in pure perception, pure experiencing of the moment, with no need to know anything except what's actually going on.

When you drive a car and are not thinking, just enjoying the experience, you do not need your memory. You drive from your experiential knowledge of driving. Some of your movements may seem to be unconscious, but the intelligence that guides the body's actions from moment to moment is a precise response to the situation. Only the novice has to think about driving.

What does it mean to live in possibilities alone?

You walk out of the door in the morning and recognise the possibility of going to work but you make no decision to go. You make your way from moment to moment, waiting at the bus stop without making any decision about whether or not you will get aboard until the moment the bus comes and you act on that possibility, or another one that has not yet been seen. Perhaps a friend will drive past and give you a lift. Perhaps someone in the queue will collapse and you will stay to help. Perhaps you have forgotten something and will have to turn back towards home.

Nothing is certain. The recognition of this is 'absence of decision'.

Life is as it is; the fact that man must live. Anything outside of it is imagination, no matter how convincing the argument to the contrary may sound.

Man must eventually realise this truth. The seeing of it is not enough. It has to be faced and lived.

Which possibility will be the fact?

The one you act on, of course — just as you are now acting on the possibility of sitting and reading or listening, with the ever-present possibility that next moment you will stop and get up.

Is there a decision? No. Only if you go outside the moment

and then you introduce the chooser and the need for a decision becomes apparent.

Choice is not a fact in the factual world of the moment. It is an appearance in a world of appearances.

Possibilities are life's way of conditioning you for possible future action. They are the only mental action that cannot be stopped.

To live in possibilities you must throw them out as they occur to you. If you don't you will begin to think and leave the moment. You have to be relentless in this.

Possibilities in themselves are very brief. You might get five or six relating to a possible action. As soon as one occurs it has to be observed as a possibility. The observer's state should be one of not knowing anything, so the possibility has to go. But what happens if the possibility is true and not thrown up by desire, is that you will briefly look at the situation and pull up any related facts in a critical evaluation of the possibility. This prepares the mind for a course of action to identify with, should the possibility become a fact. You then throw the whole lot out and revert to the state of knowing nothing: if you do not you will think.

Where there are several possibilities you will find a couple of them persist. So you examine them each time they come up to see if any new facts have emerged. And then throw the whole lot out again — no matter how much you are tempted to think about them.

You have to keep the different possibilities apart in this way. When the moment of action occurs you will act on one of them. There will be no conflict and no choice in the moment.

Or, before the moment for action, you might notice that all but one possibility has vanished; and then you may feel that you have come to a decision.

The world of appearances is a world of choice.

Is your life not based on the premise that you have a choice in just about everything?

If you say yes to this, you live in a world of appearances and not in the fact.

If you see life as it is you will see there is no choice at all for individual minds. Then any choice is merely apparent.

You might think that calling it 'a world of appearances' is the same as saying it doesn't really exist. But obviously the world, and all the objects in it, does exist. So it is not a question of whether the world exists, but whether you the chooser exist. If we take you away, what is left lives in the moment where there is no choice; the world goes on exactly as it is. And you go on, although now you see things as they really are and not through the warfare of choice, which is nothing more than the clash of powerful desires.

If you cannot accept that in truth there is no choice, I have to say that while you choose to accept or not accept you can never know the truth.

The question surely is: How do I rid myself of the chooser in me?

Only action gets rid of the chooser. Talking and thinking are not right action unless you are looking for the fact. They are dreaming; it is only in dreaming that there appears to be choice. Still, the waking dream does exist in most people as an appearance and you have to face that fact. But when you face it in yourself and take action (by never thinking or talking outside the fact) the chooser disappears. Only then do you know choicelessness.

beyond dreaming

THE DREAM-WORLD is the world of memory.

It is here that we exist as dreaming while asleep. And it is here that we exist as thinking — dreaming while awake.

Memory is the environment of the mind. The mind's world is thinking and talking outside the fact of the moment. In this way, as a waking dream, the mind enters the world where we take action, the actual world.

Mind is not a fact. It is an illusion, a wispy web of imagined relationship creating personal circumstances, involvement and limited individual responsibility; a reaction of reasons, explanations and excuses.

Let us start to look at how perception works without mind. The mind will say this is absurd; mind cannot go beyond itself. But if you have reached this point in yourself you will recognise the truth of it; you are getting ready to switch over permanently from the fluctuating principle of mind. For that is what developing consciousness, or life, is all about.

Perception, physicality and memory are the three 'environments' of man; three planes of existence.

Perception is a fact. Memory is a fact. And so is the body. When these three are all that functions in man, mind dissolves or is transcended. This can only be understood really by experiencing it. The state is beyond comprehension or words. Yet it is experienced whenever you are simply being or living in the moment.

When man is talking or thinking he is very seldom responding to the challenge of the moment. When pure perception is realised, man lives in the moment and responds only to its challenge.

To illustrate the subtlety of this:

If you were to ask a question such as 'What is your attitude to suicide?' a person operating from mind can and certainly will give an answer. But if you asked me I would have to reply in the moment; 'Attitudes are of the mind, an accumulation of yesterdays, so the question cannot be answered from a place of pure perception.'

If you rephrased the question and asked 'Is suicide right or wrong?' I would have to say: 'Suicide is a fact, like rain is a fact, so how can it be wrong?'

A fact is a fact because it exists, not because it is right or wrong. Mind is the evaluator of right or wrong. Perception sees the fact. Mind moves in as a judgment of it. This creates an hallucinatory world, an awake dream, overwhelming in its fake reality. But it does not change the fact. Suicide is the fact.

Next you might ask: 'Does suicide retard or check a person's advancement in consciousness?'

I reply: 'Everything that happens is right or it could not happen. So how can suicide be less of an aid to advancement than anything else? Suicide is only death.'

You will notice that the conversation is becoming exasperating, useless. There is no judgment, so there are no answers; only facts.

Facts are not at all satisfying. This is because man looks for answers where there are none. He does this all the time. Most conversation is therefore empty judgment and speculation, a strangely satisfying but never-ending fairy-tale world of meaningless words. As soon as you look for the fact, the conversation dies, becomes an absurdity, a talking dream for sleep-drugged men and women.

The suicide question has meaning only when it is a challenge of the moment. It is not a challenge to ask you what you would do. You do not know — unless you are so deeply grained with habitual thinking that you are as tiresome and predictable as a machine.

If you phone me and say your friend is about to commit suicide — 'What should I do?' — I will respond. But in what way I cannot tell you now.

If you march up to me and say you're going to commit suicide, I will respond. But again, until the moment, I cannot say what I will do. I might tell you to go ahead and kill yourself. I do not know.

You might say: 'I wouldn't tell anyone to kill themselves! I would try to stop it.' It's still your mind talking. The fact is you do not know what you would do. It is all possibility.

By not uttering absurdities, not thinking them; by denying yourself the opiate and comfort of the mass under-developed consciousness, you live the life of truth and you by-pass the dreaming mind.

Mind is all that talk and speculation.

Mind has no actual existence except as a reactive principle.

In sleep, coma, or under anaesthesia the mind appears to withdraw or vanish. But that is only the appearance. The brain is constantly registering the body's response to the environment and receiving signals from the physical senses. In sleep and the other levels of unconsciousness the brain's responses to the physical world are dulled or deadened and the impact of the physical environment is correspondingly diminished. So actually the world withdraws, recedes or vanishes.

The memory then takes over as the dominant source of data and provides the sleep environment; a second-hand version of the waking experience — a dream.

Sleepiness occurs when the world-creating sensory signals received by the brain are slowed down. Conversely, the more the signals are speeded up the more we feel awake, 'alive'.

While we are asleep the slow arrival of the signals creates a reduced actual environment. The frame of reference for perception is reduced to memory plus the slight sensation of the idling sensory system which keeps us linked to the world, or 'still alive' as we know it. But perception is constant, so as one environment diminishes or recedes (as in sleep or death) another arises in its place. In sleep or unconsciousness this is the memory or dream environment which now becomes the dominant experience.

Awareness is the perception of the significance of a particular environment. When the sensory signals are speeded up and we feel more awake, the potential of our awareness is also increased; its effectiveness in actuality depending on the absence of trying and wanting.

The world of actuality is a low-frequency creation. The low-frequency creates motion from which flow distance and time. If the speed or frequency of the sensory signals is increased beyond a certain level they exceed the capacity of normal sense-experience. The result is that the actual world and objects in it begin to dissolve. High frequency signals eventually reach a state of activity where motion itself disappears, and along with it time and distance. This is the beginning of non-formal environments of pure energy.

We dream in memory in terms of what we already know. The story lines are dictated by three main stimuli:

— low frequency sensory signals (touch-feeling, heat and cold, noise, etc.) that continue to impinge on memory and trigger associative dreaming;

— stored or suppressed emotion;

— high frequency pulses which are responsible for the 'creative' element in dreaming.

Our prophetic or creative dreams originate deep within us in the form of a pulse of energy. This energy has no means of expression in man except through roughly related data in the memory. We can only dream or think in terms of what we have already experienced. As memory consists of the past or the old, reality has to express the new or the future in these second-hand materials. So we dream in old, familiar terms, even though the situations may seem to be new.

At times however, we carry with us into waking consciousness the sensation of the energy behind the words and pictures we remember. This is much closer to the truth in us, although as soon as we translate the energy into words or concepts by thinking, talking or writing, it is immediately distorted and no longer new. The sensation is timeless; by uttering it we bring it into time.

Because I speak and write from the same place it follows that what I write is already old and distorted; even though what I am saying is relatively new. But if you do not try to think about what you have been reading, if you experience the energy behind what I say and do not utter or express it, you touch the consciousness that produced it.

Nothing really new can come out of the past; only reaction or modification. But it is undeniable that something uses the familiar forms in a perpetually original way to express the new, as the skill or genius of the painter uses the limited colours of the palette to create a work of art. The source of this creativity must be beyond the words, images and concepts stored in the memory. The new must arise in a state of stillness, when there is no ideal, no sought-after object, no conforming to a standard, no predetermined plan — because that is the condition of sleep. Only in the absence of trying, wanting, thinking, talking, attitudes and concepts is there creation — freedom of expression and response.

A re-creation is a workmanlike, clever or skilled combination of forms in the memory; it emerges as a copy of what has been before. A creation, or work of art, is also a combination of forms and relationships but it produces the new, the masterpiece.

What is the hidden ingredient that distinguishes the Rembrandt portrait, the Henry Moore sculpture, the Mozart Concerto from the work of an expert copyist? What is inspiration, genius? It is pure perception acting through the other two environments in man — memory and physical sensation, of which memory is the lesser or most base.

The true inspiration of genius is the sensation of the body, below all words, attitude, desire and emotion.

Pure sensation is a note struck by reality.

Because memory is the environment of the mind, which is an accumulation of the individual's reactions, it is a completely subjective, narrow and exclusive world.

When perception goes behind memory, deeper into man, it is in an environment where man loses his individuality as mind-memory-emotion and becomes the new experience of sensation-knowledge-love. In the absence of the old individuality, with its personal history, a new sense of individuality is experienced with tremendous impact. This is the rebirth that mystical and esoteric teachings aspire to.

pure perception

PERCEPTION IN US is an indescribable absolute and we would not be aware of it except that it 'appears' in an environment or 'world'.

Being absolute, it is not individual. There is no individual perception as there is a 'you' or a 'me'. It is all the perception.

If man would only grasp it, perception is all there is; containing within itself, now, all its own worlds, simultaneously. However, we have to approach the truth of it from duality, which is difficult enough anyway.

Our impression that perception is individual is created by our frame of reference. Our frame of reference is the sensory system of our individual bodies, together with all the data it throws up. No matter what you imagine, or how abstract or abstruse you might think any thought is, it is still a modification of experience reported by the senses. You cannot think outside this frame of reference, which contains everything you know that can be extracted from memory as bits of information.

While you remain within this frame of reference you are the frame, the limitation imposed by limited knowledge; you are not the unlimited, unframed, data-free perception that upholds all the references.

The data is mainly stored in two layers or aspects of memory, words and feelings — limitations. It is not the perception that is limited but the senses and the data-frames which arise from them.

The perception in us is capable of perceiving any environment or world now. It is in fact perceiving the most abstract worlds of energy at this moment. But we are not aware of it because we are identified with the body's sensory frame of reference and its values.

Man is always the limitation that he puts on himself. The fact that he regards himself as 'man' is one of the elementary limitations confining him.

What is man?

A body? A mind?

While man accepts these limitations he remains a body/mind. And that becomes his environment. The interaction between body and mind is what he calls his circumstances, which become the limited experience of life — man's world.

Man must rise above mind, above circumstance, so that his perception is aware of his body and its actions as the unfoldment of itself. Like driving a car, it requires no involvement. When the perception is totally uninvolved in the action, its environment is a world of fact and freedom, without any effort or trying.

When man reaches this perception his next advance in consciousness will be to rise above the worlds of form and actuality to exist in pure energy or perceptive space.

Before going further, it is necessary to understand something of the significance of space. Its metaphysical and real equivalents are the key to perception and higher experience.

No object can exist in actuality without space. There would be no sunsets, no smiles, no music, no talking, no thinking;

we could not even masticate our food. There would be no relationship at all. Existence as we know it, even perception, would seem to disappear.

You must be sure to grasp this: the word you read, or note you hear, exists only because of the space between the words or notes.

Indeed, it can even be said that space is the Creator, or at least the sustainer, of the shape of matter; and also of the beauty of its relationships.

What makes a cup a successful vessel? Its substance or the space in it?

Is the beauty of a piece of sculpture in the shape of its form? Or is it in the shape of the space?

How much of a painting or photograph is space?

Is not the drama of a situation the space between two or more wills, the tension and excitement, the narrowing of the gap?

Is not agreement the absence of space?

And the absence of space, the end of striving?

And the end of striving, the end of creation?

The characteristics of space are its absence of resistance, its creative stillness and its action-full nothingness.

Space is action performing as 'matter' and motion.

Matter is a name given by the imagination to the unimaginable impact of sense-perception on 'nothing'. Matter, actually, is not perceivable by us. All we perceive is form.

Form consists of space right down to the atom, which eventually disappears into energy, which is still another form of space.

So the world moves and has its being as form in space.

What is form?

Form is the corruption of space itself, a piece of space twisted by time.

There is no time in space. Space is absolute. Time is not. Time is relative to velocity, therefore dependent on motion. Space is dependent on nothing.

'Nothing' is perception, timeless and motionless.

Space then is the condition of perception; or else they are identical.

reality

WHAT CAN WE KNOW about reality? Nothing really; although we can discover what it is not, and therefore where it begins.

To begin with, there can be no motion in reality. Motion is relative, dependent on objects, space and time; anything dependent for its existence on something else cannot be real. So motion is not real; although it is actual.

Looking at motion more closely we see that every structure in the creation is in motion, within and without. The universe, the solar system, the earth, and every object on earth including everything that appears to be motionless is composed of atoms moving at tremendous speeds. Actually everything is in motion — is motion. Therefore nothing is real.

Everything is different every moment. Nothing has real individual existence, except perhaps the ultimate all-encompassing 'structure', life itself. The nuclear physicists have proved this 'absence of reality'. They have found that the position and speed of an object cannot be fixed at the same instant; if you assess the speed you cannot fix the position, and vice versa.

It is an actual world we live in, not a real one.

What is the only real thing in the world? What is the essence and totality of life, the thing that creates, delays, solves all problems;

the thing that contains all possibilities yet selects the fact of the moment — and never moves?

Action.

The appearance of reality in the world is action.

This world, the actuality, ends with action.

The world of actuality is produced by action plus motion. If we take motion away we will be able to see what action really is.

Motion is the difference between time and position.

Time is succession; position in space plus object.

So motion is succession plus space plus object.

Take away these three and what remains has to be 'real action', the significance of motion.

What is left of our world when you take away time, space and all objects?

Nothing.

But something does remain — the observer. So it is more correct to say that actuality disappears. No matter what you remove you are always there.

So the observer is the action.

To grasp the significance of all this we must look at what the observer is.

The observer is as nothing in relation to actuality.

So what is real begins with the apprehension of nothingness.

I said that the observer is action. To find out what that means, let's bring back the actuality and see what happens between the world and the observer.

For the observer to remain as nothing, what happens will have to fulfil three conditions. It must be motionless. It must be out of time; that is, instantaneous. And for it to be true you must be able to experience it.

What happens is perception.

Perception is timeless and motionless action.

What about the observer or perceiver?

There is none. There is only perception. In this reality there is no perceiver, no individual 'I' as the mind knows it.

In reality you are timeless, immortal, conscious, motionless action — as you are now, if you could just perceive and be.

If you want an actual existence as an observing or perceiving individual, you must perform in the world of thinking and dreaming. Thinking, like everything actual, is motion. When you think, the motion takes place in memory — as evaluation, judging, owning, worrying, naming and all that keeps you out of the moment where reality is.

Memory, as we have seen, is where we dream while asleep; and thinking is dreaming while awake. In thinking we are closer to actuality; in sleep we are closer to reality.

As the memory arises from the actuality, so actuality must arise from reality. In other words, reality must substantiate this world. It must be here now, if it can be perceived. But as it lies behind appearance and motion it is extremely subtle and fine, a significance beyond the comprehension of sense-perception.

Reality is in your head. But you can never know what it is because you use your physical senses to know that you have a head.

Your head and the whole sense-perceived world is in the reality — in you — but it has no real existence. It is all the actual existence of our world of action and motion perceived through the senses.

There is no real, outside world, only an appearance of it, an actuality.

Every world or environment, including the physical body and the dreamworld of memory, is within perception itself — which is you, purified of wanting and trying.

Perception, at this moment, is recreating your environment in your head from the information received by your senses as nerve-signals. No signals, no physical experience: that means unconsciousness or death.

Unconsciousness, irrespective of how it is induced, is a response to a signal or command from reality within.

Signals from reality are communicated by pulses of 'anti-matter'. (Do not allow the mind to interfere and produce questions. Keep reading.) These pulses are potentials or possibilities and appear in two ways.

A pulse from reality rises up and strikes your memory (the dream world). It throws up the concept stored there that most closely approximates to the pulse's real significance.

Or: a pulse directly enters the world, the actuality, by travelling out along your perception as your attention. It strikes an object or relationship in the actual world, then rebounds into your memory as an associated suggestion.

Actuality is the world of physical form.
Reality is the world of perceptive space-energy.
All worlds in-between are a mixture of both.

Actuality is the world of the body, not the mind. Reality should beam straight through into actuality as a harmony of action and pure perception, but it cannot do so while man's mind stands in the way like a dirty window.

The mind is the corruption that pollutes the pure perception and creates the intervening world of disharmony. It is man's shackle. Yet it is the easel of his frame of reference and only through the mind can man reach the point where he can begin to go beyond it.

Actuality arises out of two facts: space and perception. So pure perception and uncorrupted space together are the experience of reality at this moment, if it can be perceived.

The corruption of space is form, so reality consists of formless space — containing, as an unexpressed energy, the actual physical world and all that will ever appear in it, along with all less-formed worlds in a unity of will, knowledge and being. This is the being of reality, a being inseparable from the pure perception that can be experienced now.

In other words, pure perception in us is the real and only being, God Almighty, or whatever you like to call it.

To summarise:

Actuality is the apparent world outside the head.

Reality is inside the head where the actuality occurs, really.

Space and the world of forms outside the head are reported to us by sense-perception.

Sense-perception is an intrinsic phase of something immeasurably vaster — pure or real perception

Pure perception is our highest potential. It is the world-creating point of reality.

Pure perception is always the same perception: the real being, watching, motionless, unmoved, indefinable, in its own formal expression of itself.

To the extent that the corruption is removed from our perception, we are this infinite, unknowable being.

about the author

EDITOR'S NOTE

In 1965 Barry Long underwent a deep and painful spiritual crisis. He was living in a stone bungalow near Almora, 4,500ft up and isolated. The place was called Chilkapita, place of the high-flying birds.

Sitting in the garden with his typewriter he had started to put into words what he'd learned about himself over the last seven years. In that time a spiritual awakening had utterly changed his life. What had happened to Barry Long, the ambitious and successful journalist, editor of a Sydney Sunday paper? Or the husband and family man in the pleasant suburban home? They were dead personalities to the earnest, solitary figure at Almora who sat still and silent on the high terrace watching the birds glide past below him.

His book would be about meditation and what he had discovered to be the false basis of human nature. It would be a way of articulating his own observations, 'a manual of self-knowledge' to inspire others on the trail of the ultimate question.

'Who are you?' he began. 'Ask yourself the question, but don't answer. Your reply will be just your opinion . . .'

He worked sporadically, but all the time the inner pressure of confusion and despair was increasing. Then, on 11 November, came the moment of truth, his mystic death or realisation of immortality. In that 'immortal moment' he participated in the living reality behind everything he was writing about.

In the following weeks he devoted himself to the book. He even wrote to a couple of publishers in London describing it as a work of great spiritual value for anyone who had started on the road of self-discovery. One replied, saying of course that the editors would need to see the manuscript.

He had realised immortality. He suddenly saw that there was no need for him to remain in India. Why not take the book to the publisher himself? He had just enough money for the fare so he sailed from Bombay with the manuscript in his bags.

Arriving in London in March a grey fog descended on his ambitions. He visited the publisher who politely recommended him to an agent. In those days, the market for spiritual literature was much less than it is today. The agent wasn't able to sell what were then an assortment of writings and re-writings by a man God-mad, or possibly just mad.

The manuscript was clearly not going to make Barry Long's fortune, so it was put aside and he went to work as a sub-editor on the London Evening News. Two years later he met a young man on the staff of the paper who was keenly interested in truth and the spiritual life. This friend, his first student, brought others and arranged a series of meetings. Barry Long was becoming a teacher.

In November 1968 he reached a new threshold of self-discovery. Sparked by contact with those around him, the intense pressure of his spiritual process produced the transcendental realisation mentioned on pages 152-3. In the weeks immediately before and afterwards, he again put his observations down in writing as he sought to articulate the new realisation both for himself and for his small circle of students.

His friend from the newspaper gathered together all his various writings, sorted them into separate manuscripts, typed them out and printed them in private editions together with a transcript of some of his talks. They were all available by late 1969 and circulated amongst his close circle.

It was not until 1982 that he began to teach publicly, at first giving meditation classes. This created a need for back-up materials and the privately printed manuscripts were re-discovered. Two were revised and published by The Barry Long Centre in London; one was about meditation, the other was 'Knowing Yourself'.

That first edition of 'Knowing Yourself' contained the material written from November 1965 to February 1966 around the time of the realisation of immortality, together with some epigrams. This second edition includes the same text without the epigrams but with some revisions and some material from the original manuscript that was not previously included. The chapter 'Impersonal Love' has been taken from notes written in 1969 and the fourth and fifth parts of the book bring into public print for the first time the material written between November 1968 and February 1969 in the heat of the transcendental realisation. These writings have been rearranged and edited, and under Barry Long's direction some terms and expressions have been deleted or changed for the sake of clarity. This edition there-fore collects together the seminal writings associated with Barry Long's early realisations and complements two other works that originated in the same period: 'Meditation A Foundation Course' and 'Wisdom and Where To Find It' (the transcript of the 1968 meetings).

It is now thirty years since Barry Long sat in the garden at Chilkapita. The refinement and actualisation of his realisation has continued day by day of course, and by living his truth for so many years he has been able to demonstrate his enlightenment to very many people on three continents. But it is in this book that his original teaching is found — his unique contribution to us, expressed here with the immediacy of the moment.

Information about other books, tapes, videos and seminars by Barry Long can be obtained from:

The Barry Long Foundation,
BCM Box 876, London WC1N 3XX England.

The Barry Long Foundation International,
Box 5277, Gold Coast MC, Queensland 4217 Australia.

In the USA or Canada call 1-800-497-1081.